WE MARRIED ADVENTURE

Cover photo by Erwin Bauer. Back cover photo by Peggy Pucci.
Cover design and book layout by Rebecca Woods.

Ninth printing, 2020

Address correspondence to:
Gap Pucci
11950 Camp Creek Road
Jackson, Wyoming 83001
307-733-6318

We Married Adventure

Together Against the Wilderness: Life in Jackson Hole, Wyoming

by

GAP PUCCI

with Hartt Wixom

Jackson Hole, Wyoming

DEDICATION

This book is dedicated first to my God and my family, Peggy and daughters Catherine and Teresa for their help and sacrifice living our way of life in the wilds of Wyoming. Without them, this book would have been impossible. Peggy has contributed much with her photographs and diary entries. I also dedicate this book to my deceased Mother and Father and dear Aunt Pauline in raising me in my faith. And to Dean and Billie Harmon for their help and inspiration.

ACKNOWLEDGEMENTS

———

Many people, mentioned herein, assisted in writing this book. I am grateful for all of them. If I, Gap, fine-tuned my guiding, horse packing and riding skills, it was from a combination of some of Jackson Hole's best outfitters, guides and mountain men, the likes of which this country will probably never see again. It is an era gone by forever!

These outdoor experts include Albert and Bert Feuz, Dr. Don MacLeod, Mardy Murie, Larry Moore, Rex Ross, Ben France, Neil Rafferty, Bob Wiley, Howard Ballew, Marion Davidson, Lou Blair, Tom Lamb, Roy Martin, and my Dad who was my first teacher. He took me on my first big game hunts. (They are all now deceased except Bert Feuz and Bob Wiley.)

It was an honor and a privilege to know them. They took the time to share their secrets about big game hunting, horsemanship and the high mountain country of Jackson Hole. I could never thank them enough for all they shared with me. I only hoped that I would be as good as they were. They carried a proud tradition of the early mountain man. I hope I made them proud of me! May our trails cross again someday!

In addition, much has come from the experiences Peggy and I enjoyed—despite our challenges and hardships—in the wilds of Wyoming. My purpose in wanting to write this book is intertwined with my desire to share those experiences and point out how they shaped our lives. In some ways, we were not really prepared for what took place, even though I had spent some time with the Army troops in Alaska and learned much about horses in Pennsylvania before moving to Wyoming. But thank goodness for the kind people of Jackson Hole who knew we must be—or had to become—rugged individualists in order to survive...and were willing to help.

The inspiration provided for this book by Hartt and Judene Wixom is much appreciated. Hartt wrote several magazine and newspaper articles and a book about my way of life. I also thank good friends Peggy and Erwin Bauer who always supported my family's love of the outdoors. The Bauers left this world a better place with their well known books and photographs of wildlife.

This book is for all who might think of moving to a country life and partaking of the experiences we encountered.

We especially pay tribute to our faith in the God whom we called on so many times.

TABLE OF CONTENTS

———+———

FOREWORD

I first met Gaspari (named after his father) "Gap" and Peggy Pucci while visiting Jackson Hole, Wyoming in 1981 with former *Outdoor Life* magazine associate editor Rich LaRocco. We were seeking big game to photograph. Erwin Bauer, Teton Village, with a world-wide reputation for outstanding wildlife photography, recommended we visit Gap and Peggy. Not only had Bauer witnessed considerable mule deer, elk, moose and bighorn sheep in Hoback Canyon near the Pucci residence, but knew him to be savvy in outdoor lore and experience. We found Bauer to be correct.

Visiting Gap and Peggy in their trophy-laden log home, it became immediately evident that this was an Italian-American man who loved the wildlife and hunting challenge of the Mountain West. Not many hunting seasons later, I joined Gap for an elk quest in his beloved Gros Ventre (Indian tribe name for "big bellies," or "always hungry" according to French trappers) wilderness and personally watched him bugle in two bulls for hunters. At his home, I admired big game heads adorning the walls; they reminded me of the hey-days of the Old West, even Buffalo Bill. I included much of his wisdom and experience on wildlife and horses in my book *Elk and Elk Hunting*.

Gap is a throwback to frontier times, not born a hundred years too late as much as forging the past century to the present. Visitors could sit by a fire and listen to him talk about his experiences in the wilds of Wyoming for hours. Many have. I have.

Pucci was not, however, born in the West. His forefathers came from Italy and settled in a suburb of Philadelphia. The culture remained Italian and with it the Catholic Church. He described his father as a strict disciplinarian, his mother as one who cooked for the entire neighborhood. (Gap said he spent most of his time in the gym to get in shape and stay out of trouble.) There was nothing in close family ties which might lead to a life in the West or the outdoors in general, even though he was early enthralled with horses and had worked for a veterinarian, Dr. Harry Steinbach of Blue Bell, Pennsylvania. But Gap began reading the outdoor magazines and the die was cast.

When he could gather enough money, Gap flew to Casper, Wyoming, after making arrangements to hunt antelope on a ranch west of town. The guide was not there to pick him up, so he talked to someone who agreed to take him out to the ranch. "I knew you'd find me sooner or later," explained the rancher, Ben France. And thus began Pucci's do-it-yourself romance with the West.

Later on in 1964, he signed on to hunt with Albert and Margaret Feuz (pronounced Fates) Ranch at Bondurant. It was here he met Peggy McClung of Kansas and Salt Lake City. Peggy had signed on to work in one of the Rocky Mountain's most reputable big game Valhallas. Gap successfully took several big game animals here on the western edge of the Wind River Mountains, but winning over the pretty girl from the city was something else. She had graduated from the University of Kansas with a major in French and Spanish and had studied the languages in France, Spain and Belgium. Why should she marry someone who would take her to an isolated cabin with no running water, no telephone, or television, or central heating, 10 miles from the nearest road?

But that was what she did.

While she learned to love the outdoors from family camping trips, Peggy had never hunted. She did, however, quickly embrace the lifestyle after marrying. She was versed in the world of fashion and design, creative arts, photography, leather work, sewing, writing of greeting cards...but now had little time to meet survival needs in Jackson Hole, Wyoming. But she found ways to adjust, and with her two daughters born in lonely Hoback Canyon, all won dozens of blue ribbons at the county fair. Although she did not revel in horsemanship (horsewomanship?), she did, with her husband, teach the girls enough, at times, to scintillate in many Teton County fairs/rodeos.

When I visited Gap in July, 1997, he had just been thrown from a colt he was attempting to saddle break. He had also received a sharp hoof blow to the head (requiring stitches) from a stallion while trying to arrange a tryst between it and one of his mares. "Part of the daily routine," he explained matter-of-factly. Gap broke many horses...but not without injury.

Fortunately for today's reader, Gap and Peggy kept meticulous diaries of their years in the wilds of Wyoming. With a deep bonding to face any and all adversity, their story is an inspiration for all who would like to depart the hassle of traffic and city confusion to live as the pioneers of the 1800s. It reminded me of an interview I had with a man who rowed his way across the Atlantic Ocean. It took five months. "What is your advice for others trying such an adventure?" I asked. He said, "You better like yourself." While the Pucci's 25-year odyssey in Granite Creek Canyon was quite different from that of sailor James Kimball, the theme he suggested was true: you better like (love?) yourself—and in this case, each other. "You'll be spending a lot of time together. Just the two of you."

Let Louis L'amour or Zane Grey write their fiction of days gone by. Gap and Peggy Pucci lived it...as much as could be done in the late 1900s. Most of their story is taken directly from their diaries. Although even the diaries of Lewis and Clark on their "Corps of Discovery" to the West in 1803-05 were cryptic enough at times to require interpretation, their biographers were sensitive enough to remain out of it as much as possible—yet do justice to the diary writers while retaining the original flavor. I shall try to do as well.

—Hartt Wixom

THE NEW WORLD OF WYOMING

Note: The first person "I" is the voice of Gap Pucci in the following pages unless otherwise indicated.

My Italian name is Gaspari Pucci but everyone has called me "Gap" since I was a teen and it is the only name I have ever used since. I came west from Pennsylvania in 1964 to hunt the elk, deer and antelope I'd read about in the outdoor magazines. That was my focus and I knew to succeed that I must get up early, hunt late and funnel all my energy in combing the high country. The thought of failure could not cross my mind, for this was to fulfill the one-time dream hunt of my lifetime. Traveling so far, I didn't want to squander the opportunity. It might be my only trip to Wyoming.

Yet, I discovered something for which I had to return to the West. Her name was Peggy. Peggy Ann McClung worked for the Albert Feuz Ranch south of Jackson Hole where I stayed for two weeks. I tried to conceal any idea that there was more on my mind than the hunt, especially from my guides Albert and Bert Feuz. But my thoughts of Peggy would not go away. I learned she had recently graduated from the University of Kansas, majoring in Spanish and

French, returning home to her parents in Salt Lake City, Utah, then answering an ad to work at the Feuz Ranch through summer and autumn. Her plan after that was to begin a career as an interpreter, wherever it took her, possibly away as far as Spain or France.

Being of Italian descent, I didn't know what impact I could have on her life. But I quickly noted she loved the wild surroundings of the ranch, located near Bondurant, as did I. Wildlife abounded and we could talk briefly in the evening about what we had both witnessed during the day: clean air, cool winds, quiet solitude, wildflowers, meadowlarks, moose, elk, antelope, deer and sheep. In the nearby high country of the Gros Ventre Mountains I heard elk bugle, that magnificent call of the wild which stirred me as much as rival bulls. Peggy seemed genuinely interested in hearing me talk of it. The more I thought about it, the more it seemed to me that we appreciated, even loved, the same things.

But was her interest in the outdoors, in wildlife, merely a superficial thing, a conversation pastime for the moment only? I learned she was born in Lawrence, Kansas, and after enrolling at the University of Kansas, her folks moved to Salt Lake City. They spent summers enjoying the outdoors but I didn't know exactly how "outdoorsy" Peggy really was. When my hunt was over at the Feuz Ranch, I had succeeded in taking a six-point bull elk, buck mule deer and antelope! They were reasons to return to this hunting Valhalla. But to be honest, there was another reason. I wrote to Peggy and was excited to find her writing back. She knew how into the outdoors I was—and very intense fascination about hunting—and here she was writing back!

Just before New Year's Eve, 1964, I flew from my home in Pennsylvania to Salt Lake City. Peggy didn't know until Dec. 31 that I was in Utah. But her voice was warm on the telephone and she invited me over. I stayed at the Hotel Utah in downtown Salt Lake City for two weeks and met her parents. At end of that time, I headed home, or at least to Chicago. Then I got to thinking things over, marched to the airline counter and traded in the rest of my ticket for a return to Salt Lake City.

We were married March 6, 1965. We made a comfortable home in the hills of Pennsylvania, but began to talk about how much we loved northwestern Wyoming. Nothing would do until we sold the comfortable farm home we were living in and wrote to the Feuz family about working in Wyoming. They lined up an interview for us at nearby Granite Ranch. I was told I couldn't be a guide during the first year, but could learn to be a packer and wrangler and if successfully learning the ropes, become a guide the next year. That's the way it worked out. In time, we also began to manage a hot springs property [for public use] owned by the U.S. Forest Service in Granite Creek Canyon. This stream was a tributary to the Hoback River, which in turn flows into the Snake River on the south end of Jackson Hole. We liked some nearby scenic property in that area which we were able to purchase that same autumn.

But we didn't really comprehend what we were getting into.

To properly manage the Springs we would have to live year-around on the property, 10 miles up Granite Creek on a long dirt road the county would not plow. We would be snowed in from November through May. Although two miles from the Springs, we would have to check daily on who was using and paying for them. We would also have to cut our own firewood, for there was only a wood stove, no central heating. With no running water, we would get our own by cutting the ice in Granite Creek and heating it in the cabin to thaw out. There was no telephone or communication with the outside world of any sort.

If we didn't plan wisely...maybe we would not survive. There would be no neighbors, or anyone to look after us if trouble should arise. "No one has ever spent a winter here," we were told. That was the scenario we faced as converts to the ways of frontier western life—and us fresh from the East, two thousand miles away.

But I looked at Peggy and she looked at me and we said we would do it. Later, we admitted to having a lump in our throats. But we knew that surely we would not be bored. We were right.

In fact, we learned very quickly that we had not just married each other but an adventure beyond our expectations. While we were not exactly city dudes, we were soon to learn about what it was like to live through the next several winters in the high mountains of Wyoming.

First order of business was to winterize an old rustic bunkhouse on the banks of Granite Creek, the entire canyon surrounded by white-capped peaks thrusting into the sky more than 11,000 feet elevation. The existing structure had cracks large enough between the logs for a skunk or badger to crawl through, let alone the howling wind. Of the snow, we measured it at 450 inches deep before the spring thaw would finally arrive. The thermometer plummeted to 50 degrees below zero that first winter. Hauling ice from the creek was no easy task, for many mornings we had to break the ice to gain enough slush to drink and wash in. Fortunately, the slope we were located on attracted the sun more each day than some gullies and hills nearby and melted the snow faster. But while we read of balmy days in Pennsylvania and Salt Lake City, we remain locked in by winter's white fastness.

It wasn't long before we found ourselves surrounded with wildlife: moose, elk, deer, black and grizzly bears, mountain lion, coyotes, timber wolves and to our pleasant surprise, Rocky Mountain bighorn sheep. I had seen a few such game animals up close in a two-year military stint to Alaska. But now the game seemed almost ready to move into the house with us. Of course, we had somewhat usurped their winter home, so we felt a desire to feed and help them in every way we could.

WE LEARN FAST—WE HAVE TO

As we prepared for our new challenge at Granite Creek, we found a few parallels with our seven years on a farm in Pennsylvania. But we found some major differences. For one thing, our new bunkhouse had one light bulb hanging from the ceiling which almost always died with the first wind; no running water, no plumbing [an outhouse only], and we had to haul water from the creek which required breaking thick ice during the winter.

My diary reads as follows:

Aug. 30, 1973: For the last 10 days we have been buying supplies for us and our dogs, ducks and squirrel. We have to be well prepared, for in November we will be snowed in...We got up at 5 a.m. and loaded up our two trucks with all gear and left Peggy's home in Salt Lake City for Wyoming. We enjoyed seeing antelope on the way but the rest was all work. We got to bed at 1:30 a.m.

Sept. 1: This morning brought the first new snow on top of the Gros Ventre [Grow Vaunt] Mountains. The range is named after a local Indian tribe found by William Jackson and other mountain men of the early 1820s. It is also the first day of the hunt for Rocky Mountain bighorn sheep! There were hunters in the mountains but I couldn't yet be one of them. There was just too much work to do.

Until the bunkhouse was brought up to living standards, we would have to live in the camper. We spent much time trying to level it on the rocky ground! We'll have to camp here about 200 yards from the hot springs until Nov. 1. Then we were able to set up camping at the bunkhouse on what is known as Granite Creek Ranch for the long winter.

This morning we saw a husband and wife about 60 years old, Bob and Roberta Hundley, and their guide, Grover Bassett, coming out of the high mountains with their saddle and pack horses. They had bagged their bighorn sheep and were very happy. The bighorn is the most prized trophy animal in the world, living at about 10,000 feet elevation on the rocky ledges and being the hardiest animal of all to reach. Its flesh is the best tasting of all wild meat in my opinion. And Wyoming, where we lived, has the largest population of Rocky Mountain bighorn sheep in North America. [Wild sheep of Alaska and northern Canada are mostly Dall and Stone sheep.]

Sept. 3, Labor Day: Our first challenge in operating the hot springs. Pretty busy. Nice weather. Also met some nice people!

Sept. 4: The Forest Service is pleased that we are living at the hot springs. They want to cooperate and work with us. A river-running guide brought his people over and had a picnic at the Springs. We stayed open until 10 p.m.

Sept. 5: Saw an archery hunter coming in this morning after elk. He backpacked up the Granite Creek trail to the north. Larry Moore, a local outfitter, took 18 horses loaded with gear into his hunting camp this morning. I'd like to be with them.

I began to repair a roof and building at the Springs. I cleaned the pool in the evening, had supper, then went for a swim.

Sept. 6: Everything went fine in the morning. Then about 1 a.m., eight to 10 cars pulled in. They were hippies and they left a mess for us to clean up in the morning. I had not expected to find hippies in western Wyoming but they found us...and it was only the beginning of trouble we would have with these people sneaking in and leaving their trash everywhere. They don't want to pay or obey any rules.

I went to Jackson, 40 miles away, and notified the U.S. Forest Service and Teton County Sheriff's Office. The next night, two sheriff deputies and I ran about 20 hippies out of the Springs. The next night we ran out some 20 more. They had discovered us en masse and we would have no end of trouble with them that autumn.

About 9:30 p.m. Peggy and I were having supper when we heard a girl scream. I ran out of the camper carrying my .38 Smith and Wesson pistol and found a man attacking a girl. I put my pistol toward the man's stomach and told him to start walking out. I put the girl in her car and she drove out in a hurry. The sheriff in Jackson later told me the girl filed rape charges against the man.

We are 10 miles back in the wilderness but having a different kind of excitement with wildlife than I'd expected in moving from Pennsylvania.

Sept. 8: No hippies today. Maybe one reason was that it snowed. It was beautiful! Everything had turned white overnight!

Sept. 9: Larry led a 25-horse pack train into the mountains where he has set up his hunting camp. Tonight at 1 a.m. I heard hippies come in as we were trying to sleep. At 3:30 a.m. I couldn't stand it anymore. I holstered my .38 and went out in my robe and hat and chased the whole damn bunch out of the area. About 18 of them. I almost had to use my pistol! I wonder now when I will have to.

Sept. 10: This morning we are tired. The first thing I do is dig out my .44 Magnum and load it. I strap it on and drive down the canyon 20 miles to the nearest phone. I leave the .38 with Peg and tell her to use it if she has to. She knows how.

Peggy had practiced with the pistol. Now we wondered if it might come in handy. We both dreaded the thought of her having to use it, but Peg was ready if necessary while I was gone. Once again, I notified the Forest Service and sheriff's office about the hippie problem.

Today is the first day of the elk hunt! A few hunters are using the hot springs. A big rainstorm hit this afternoon. I wonder if the hippies will come tonight. We are ready!

Sept. 11: I drove to the place where I could try a field radio the Forest Service suggested in case of emergency. Could not get through to Jackson because of high mountains. Later in the day, while working, we saw two of Larry's men coming by with a pack string loaded with four bull elk!

Tonight Peg and I were invited to supper and nice evening with our friends, Janet Moore, Dr. and Mrs. MacLeod and children and Ted, a hunting guide. Wonderful people!

Sept. 12: Janet gave us some fresh milk from their cow to drink. An outfitter from Afton brought some hunters to the hot springs. At 11 p.m. I ran a man out of the springs with my pistol.

I was contacted by a woman who said a wrangler and packer working for Oral Wheeler had broken his leg and Oral wanted me to go to work for them. But I cannot leave here as I am obligated to the Forest Service to stay here and run Granite Hot Springs as agreed in our lease with them. I'd hoped to get a chance to help Larry at his camp later on.

Sept. 13: Peg drove to Jackson. She had loads of laundry to do and errands to run. Saw Larry's wrangler packing out a good moose and another elk. From Larry's camp so far, they've taken five elk and a moose in five days of hunting. That has to be superb game country up there on the mountain above us. Peggy got back late, both of us tired and sleepy.

Sept. 14: This evening a hunter offered me a moose he had just shot. I refused it. I like to get my own meat. Forest Service came by and we looked over a spot to put another barrier to keep people out after hours.

Tonight, a surprise. A young couple I let swim free one night came by to pay me and say Goodbye. They were going south. Nice kids but a little dirty looking, long hair...yet, they did right and I respect them for that.

Sept. 15: Today, Dr. MacLeod and I got to talking about a moose some hunters shot and left behind to spoil. We rode up the trail and found it lying there in front of us, gutted but not tagged. So, Doc and I quartered the moose and lay it on a log, and covered it with pine boughs to keep it cool. Doc called the fish and game department so they could get the meat out and donate it to an institution. He also gave them the auto license number of the hunter who illegally killed the moose and left the meat to waste. The moose weighed 1,000 lbs. Met Jim Mauer, a very nice guy from the Forest Service. Helped two hunters load a horse on a trailer.

Sept. 16: A game warden arrived, asked for a description of the moose poacher and said he would track him down! Doc, his grandsons and I arrived with horses to pack out the moose meat.

Larry's cook came down and said they had bagged another elk and a moose from the camp and others could have scored had they been able to shoot. Later, Larry's guide packed out a sixth elk. This was one hunting area I had to see! Weather was beautiful for repairing the cabin [bunk house]. Hope this continues.

Sept. 18: Larry says many of the hunters are leaving litter all along the trail. He grew tired of picking up after them. The game warden gave us a hind quarter of the moose which was illegally shot. He will send us more!

Ran out more hippies. They never have any money except for beer. I carry a pistol now constantly. Peggy helped Janet at the ranch and then went for a horseback ride with her.

Sept. 19: I noticed later that I left this page blank. Things must be slowing down. But it probably won't last long.

ALONE WITH THE SNOW
Peggy's Journal Entries

Nov. 19, 1973: It is so still, so quiet. Everyone is gone—everyone but me, as a matter of fact, right now, as Gap has gone to Pinedale with Larry Moore to help load hay. So I am alone for several days.

The snow is between three and four feet deep. The sun came out today for the first time in a long while. I ventured out on snowshoes. I did not go far but far enough to appreciate the beauty of the day and the serenity of the scene. It was enough to bring tranquility to an otherwise melancholy mood. I saw a cow and calf moose. I also saw tracks of deer and coyotes, so they must be near the bunk house. (Gap: Peggy will tell all that she is a social person but she is living alone now and will need to make a major adjustment in her life. She is learning not only how to be alone but take advantage of solitude.)

I am curious why the sounds of the stream harden and soften. Is it due to air currents, or fluctuations in the stream's water level?

This morning it seems evident that I was hearing snow slides or avalanches far up the canyon, coming down with a roaring sound.

The Clark's nutcrackers [camp robbers] are busy working on the meat carcasses hung to cool on the outbuildings. The icicles are dripping rapidly in the sunlight off the roof of the outbuildings and now and then a chunk crashes down. This echoes in the air and the varying breezes often make the only sound to be heard. This Fall has been a busy and interesting one. I was so busy running back and forth at the ranch it seemed that I could not observe Autumn's passing as I would like to have.

I met many fine people and passed many happy hours with them.

We spent many days in the camper cramped up before moving to the bunk house, but endured the lack of space as was necessary. It was like being in a can of sardines. But keeping busy, it wasn't really so bad. We'd tend the hot springs, go to the ranch, take care of the animals, talk to people and hunters and go on "little walks." We had thought most of our enjoyment would be in the scenery and wildlife and that has been appreciated; but it has also been the people we have met who made this past few months so especially enjoyable.

One thing which also made life less lonely with Gap away was Butch, our pet squirrel. My diary entry for Nov. 19 reads, Little Pinky Poo was always fun to come home to. Our little one was always eager to play...then settle down in my arms or crawl in my shirt to cuddle up and sleep. We carried him, pen and all, to the hot springs, that he could enjoy the day too. I always loved to get my hands on that furry little guy. The sparkle in his eyes and cute, gentle ways always enlightened my day.

Then on Nov. 9 at 2 a.m. the Lord took him from us. What a turmoil it was for us…precious was the light in his eyes…I longed to reach out and have him come back to us—to touch his soft, sweet fur, to have him cuddle up and tuck his little nose under my chin again. All we have now is sweet, tender memories…and a lesson in love learned. The little one was more than a pet to me—for through him I could see God.

Nov. 20: As the sun goes down and the mountainside darkens, the 1973 hunting season comes to an end. So that should prevent snowmobiles from getting stuck along the trail past Granite Pool. It will be very quiet now [with no more hunters' snowmobiles].

It got quite cold last night. I got up at 2 a.m. and at 6:45 a.m. again to start the fire. It was minus 5 degrees at 7 a.m. It was very clear last night. And this morning the most beautiful frost flakes were everywhere outside. Some were complex flakes as much as 1-2 inches in diameter.

Did not see any moose or other animals today—but I did not go far from the bunk house. I tried to get the carpeting pieces down on the floor to make the place warmer.

There is one large national feed grounds northeast of Jackson and several state winter refuges for the elk in the general region.

Nov. 27: How fast a week has gone! Gap did not get back last week until about 1 p.m. Thursday, Thanksgiving Day. I was beginning to think it would be the first Thanksgiving I ever spent alone... we went to Dr. MacLeod's for dinner. It was such a lovely, beautifully served dinner. We spent the night at the Moores. Saturday we went with all of them in the family "bus" to Pinedale for the day. While Gap and Larry loaded hay, the boys went rabbit hunting and the ladies...we just messed around. Later, we snowmobiled, pulling all of the kids on skis.

With the snow piling up, we could hardly get to the ranch anymore with our truck. Snowmobiles and snowshoes would be our sole transportation (from bunk house 10 miles to the highway) rest of the winter. So, we weren't really snowed in yet, but the snow was piling higher every week. After returning from Pinedale, I cooked some of the jackrabbits the boys shot. It was the first time I'd cooked jackrabbit. Made a stew. Not bad. I thought it better than cottontails. So did Gap.

The elk have by now moved out of the area—though most hunters did not know it. The big animals have already migrated toward the Camp Creek feeding grounds.

The bunk house is pretty comfy now. Yesterday, I attached the new rigging to our snowshoes and we tried out my pair. Can get around pretty well in them now.

On Dec. 3 we tried to take our truck to the highway to get into town and do some Christmas shopping, but it was a mistake. We couldn't get through and we had a great deal of trouble. We went back to the snowmobiles, cold on a windy day, to reach the highway 10 miles away. My diary reads: "We got there!"

Later, the snowmobile began losing power and Gap took it apart to see if he could find the difficulty. He put it back together and it still wouldn't work right, so he snowshoed much of 20 miles to the nearest phone to call town for help. Gap did get through with the truck on occasion by putting chains on both front and back tires. At that time we had no four-wheel drive.

Dec. 8: Our snow machine is repaired and running fine now. Much more power. Sure am relieved about that.

Dec. 9-15: Have been baking Christmas cookies all week long, about six different kinds. Making the pizzelles [Italian waffles] was a lot of fun—the first time I've used my new iron. The old one had to be hand held over a coal stove.

Dec. 16: Larry, Don and Scott Moore came in the afternoon on their new snow machines. Another nice day. We had a good visit. And they brought us some ranch pork! We really appreciated this, as our larder was filled mostly with moose meat and there was little variety in our diet when we couldn't get to the store for weeks at a time.

Dec. 17: Carried water today, cut wood and finished the Christmas baking—plus peanut brittle.

Dec. 18: Went to the hot springs to give it a clean out this afternoon. Sure gets slick and slimy! Had a nice soak as the pool was refilling, then hustled on home before dark. Just before bedtime this evening I stepped outside and saw a strange light turn toward the lower bridge. I watched it 'till it disappeared, then told Gap. We boarded the snowmobile together and took off in the night to investigate. Ski tracks! Gap followed the trail into the jack pines 'till he found the people. They were OK. They had decided to spend the night at a summer cabin rarely used on a site leased from the Forest Service. Back again to a warm cozy fire and bed!

I've been asked about whether the hippies returned as often as in warm weather. No. But there was always that chance. The Spring's water was still as warm as ever, steaming a thick mist in the December air, as does water when warmer than the surrounding air. But it was cold getting in and out and access was now almost entirely by snowmobile and snowshoe, or part way with mighty tough truck drive with chains. Gap and I decided it was getting too harsh for hippies. After all, what they wanted was an easy life. So, at least for awhile anyway, I didn't have to pack a pistol day and night. Cold weather has its advantages!

I also thought about life in Pennsylvania. We had 40 acres there but here we feel like all outdoors is our home. We can look to mountain peaks dozens of miles away and know there is no one between. It all belongs to the federal government but in a way, it seems like ours.

Dec. 20-21: Rose early. Twelve degrees below zero. I bundled up well, leaving after sunrise by myself with two bundles of laundry and a box of cookies for the Forest Service in Jackson. Had dinner with MacLeods and stayed overnight. When I got back to the trailhead for our place, I discovered the Highway Department had plowed out the parking area near the highway. Did a good job too.

When we had a lot to haul, we began to use a sleigh drawn by the snow machine. Sometimes as we glided around at sunrise or sunset, I would stop to reflect on the calm, beautiful scenery passing by us...what a lovely ride, what a lovely winter. What an experience!

I don't remember singing "Jingle Bells" out loud but I sort of hummed it in my mind as we skimmed over the trail on glistening snow.

Dec. 22-23: It cleared up and grew sunny again. But there was plenty of snow on the ground. Of a white Christmas we were assured.

Dec. 24: The afternoon of Christmas Eve is here...fixed up the old ski boots that Dr. MacLeod gave us. Time to try them out. Going to bake some bread this afternoon. Tonight Gap and I will have pizza and our own little Christmas Eve. We'll open our gifts and prepare to hitch up the sleigh and head for town tomorrow for Christmas Day with the MacLeods, Moores and Albert/Margaret Feuz.

As another month has passed, we have of course, had plenty of snow. But I am a little disappointed we don't have more. It has not snowed as much as it has "settled in" this month. But who knows what January has in store!

And what will the New Year 1974 bring?

CHRISTMAS IN WYOMING

Peggy: Christmas—our alarm went off very early as we intended to get up and leave early...but not so. It was snowing already at daylight and rapidly increased in intensity until it became blizzard-like. It was coming down so rapidly you could not see and the wind (which is rare here) was blowing too. After we saw this, we went back inside and decided we had better not try to go. We both felt disappointment. So, I went about the bunk house doing a few miscellaneous things and soon I noticed out the window that snow had slowed.

After we bundled up and started out in the snowmobile hooked up to the sleigh, we found it was still blizzardly although we could see enough for travel. But the snow was thick and we started getting very wet. We came across another family trying to get through the snow and pulled them awhile until we came to a drift when we had to get out and push. Finally we got to town 38 miles away and were able to spend the holiday with our friends.

We were going first to visit Albert and Margaret Feuz, where I first met Gap when he came west hunting. They have a lovely home and we had Christmas dinner there. We spent the evening with the MacLeods. We stayed the night with the Moores. We concluded there is nothing more valuable than tried and true friends and we were extremely blessed in this regard. We had many friends in Pennsylvania and at my home in Salt Lake City, of course. But there is nothing like the closeness you feel in a frontier atmosphere, all helping one another.

When we got back the day after Christmas it was 25 degrees inside the bunk house. It took quite a long time to get the heavier wood burning and warm the place up, using both of the stoves. Fortunately, we had labored earlier in the Fall for many hours to gather enough wood for the winter...or at least we hoped we had, for there would be much more winter ahead. We learned the truth: this Wyoming high country held at least eight months of it!

I was disappointed to find my 40-year-old "Christmas cactus" frozen. The whole plant had not been affected, but 50 per cent of the "foliage" is lost. Not only will my favorite plant not bloom this year but it will be lucky to survive at all! By late evening, the bunk house was again warm and cozy—and we fell comfortably and tiredly into our bed and fell fast asleep.

•••

Gap—Nov. 9: Little Butch, our pet squirrel that we raised from an infant in Pennsylvania, took a turn for the worst: we lost him at 2 a.m. He was 2 ½ years old. We'll miss him. He was a God-given bundle of love and joy, a precious gift of wildlife that we felt we were chosen to have—and he to have us! We buried him on the Moore Ranch under a pine tree which will again make him a part of nature and God's world.

Nov. 11: Went with Larry again to take more horses to the Pinedale ranch. We saw a good bull moose, some cows and a calf moose, big buck deer with does, and about 100 antelope.

Nov. 12: I went to the Forest Service office and was given a deputy badge to wear by Jim Mauer, District Ranger, as I am the only man covering what happens in this part of the Teton Forest.

Nov. 13: Larry finished outfitting hunters in Granite Creek and will winter in Jackson with his wife and family. Janet went back to town for the winter. When Doc MacLeod goes, Peggy and I will be the only humans left in this part of the Teton Forest and the first to ever winter in the deep snows of Granite Canyon.

Nov. 15: We now have over three feet of snow. Bob, one of the guides, came in to get his three horses out. Granite Creek is getting very quiet. And snowed in.

Nov. 16: I used a snowmobile and sleigh to cut and move

firewood today from the forest. Peggy and I, Brave, our German shepherd, Stoney, our hounds, two ducks, the Moore's ranch cat and one wild [feral] cat are the only ones left for now. Had elk meat and barley for supper. Our freezer is full. We have elk, moose, deer, beef, pork, and lamb meat. The boys went rabbit hunting. I shot one later in the day that made three weighing 6-7 lbs. each. I skinned and quartered them. Saw 11 moose. It is still snowing.

Nov. 26: Went down to Granite Creek and hauled 55 gallons of water! Went into the forest and cut a 150-foot high tree for firewood. Got back at dark, the bottom of my pants frozen stiff. Coyotes were howling as I left the forest. Peg made jackrabbit stew for supper; it was very good, like beef stew. I put out a salt block for the moose. We can watch them from the cabin window now.

Nov. 28: Went the 10 miles up to Hot Springs to drain and clean pool. Peg and I took a hot bath with four feet of snow surrounding us and air temperatures at 20 degrees.

On Nov. 29, when I went into the forest to cut firewood, I came across the tracks of a young cow elk we'd seen the day before which looked weak. Followed the tracks to be sure coyotes did not attack and kill her. Followed her for quite a while and decided she would make it, as she had already traveled quite a ways. An adult elk can manage quite easily against a single coyote...but if weak and surrounded by a pack, well, only God could help the poor elk then! Cut down another big tree and as darkness closed in, the coyotes began to howl once again.

Dec. 7: Pearl Harbor Day! Traveled 30 miles to make a phone call! Got good pictures of a big bull moose in the Hoback Canyon. On the way back, went to Hot Springs and guess what? Found the weakened cow elk living near the springs.

During this time, a friend, Terry, traveled 40 miles from Jackson to bring us a new clutch for the snowmobile. Afterward, I loaded a bale of hay for the injured elk at the Hot Springs. I feel good now that the elk will have feed! Got back at dark. Peggy had supper ready and warm water on the table.

Dec. 9: Peggy's been writing Christmas cards. I went up to the Hot Springs and some snowmobilers and skiers had used the pool. I took a 50-lb. block of salt to the springs for the elk.

Dec. 10: A photographer from *American Farms* magazine in Alabama showed up. Had lunch with us and had a nice visit. Took pictures of Jim Scott, Peg and myself for magazine.

Dec. 11: Mom's birthday. I went into the forest to cut trees for firewood. Went to the Hot Springs and soaked my sore back. Also put another bale of hay for the lonesome elk.

Dec. 14: it has been snowing for the past three days. We now have another 20 inches of powder on the ground. Rode out on my snowmobile 10 miles to take our Christmas cards to be mailed. The going was tough, as the new snow made visibility poor. On the way back, I saw an ermine [weasel] in its white winter coat. I tried to photograph it but the animal moved too fast.

I came upon two Forest Service employees whose snowmobile had broken down. I then opened a trail and helped them get out. I also helped Jim Scott's man get a belt back on his snowmobile. Got home at dark. Peg had baked Christmas cookies.

Dec. 15: I cut wood and shoveled snow and then went to Hot Springs. Broke some trails. Came across the elk's tracks but did not see her. I did not follow her as the snow is very deep and I did not want to scare her. This time of year, of course, pushing an animal in deep snow could use up the little fat reserves remaining and push the creature to the last edge of her strength. If that didn't kill her, she would be extremely vulnerable to the coyotes.

Dec. 24: This morning I hauled in 50 gallons of water as I do every Monday morning. Took my weekly bath at the hot springs. That evening we opened our Christmas presents we received some nice presents that we can use.

Dec. 25: Christmas, the day we celebrate the birthday of our

Lord! Yes, we're having a white Christmas. On our way out to the highway on my cross country skis, I could see that Mrs. Blackbourne on her skis was in a state of exhaustion and near hysteria. [She was one of those who had leased summer cabin sites from the Forest Service and was staying there for the holidays. The Blackbournes used the lower part of the same snow-laden road we did to reach the highway.] I put her on the snowmobile as Peg rode in the sleigh. We took her to the highway with our machine bucking high winds and deep snow, getting stuck near Little Granite. They should never have tried to get out during a snow storm! Lucky I came along.

We got her out to the road where there was a vehicle and were presumably able to enjoy a Merry Christmas. Looking back on it, we might have saved her from hypothermia or frostbite, or something worse that day by going out on a day when we probably shouldn't have.

Mrs. Blackbourne's state of mind also reminded Peggy and me once again of the need for careful preparation during the winter months in this part of the West. Indeed, the mountains of western Wyoming are no place to be careless, or unprepared at any time of year.

IT GETS WILD

Gap—Dec. 26: We saw nine mountain sheep pawing in the snow for food. I photographed them and enjoyed seeing them. We are lucky to have them at all!

Saw our yearling elk that was hurt and that we were feeding. Seems she made it down to the Hoback River [where food is more plentiful] and seems fine; but we'll miss her.

Today, Larry started his horse-drawn sleigh rides through the National Elk Feeding grounds north of Jackson, largest elk feed lot in the world!

Dec. 27: Woke up this morning to a new snowstorm; already six inches has fallen and no letup in sight. Went up to the Hot Springs in the afternoon, visibility poor, as we now have 15 inches of new snow on top of four feet. On the way back, my front head-light went out as the storm got worse. It was a whiteout and I could not see without my front light. Here I was miles from the ranch and not able to go...fumbling around trying to find the trouble as I stood in snow up to my waist. I had just decided to walk back when I remembered I had a dim flashlight in the tool compartment.... With the flashlight in one hand and steering with the other, I proceeded, hardly able to see through the furious snowstorm.

Slowly, by memory, I guided the snow machine in the direction of the ranch, getting bogged down in waist-high drifts. When I got within a quarter-mile of the ranch, I could see that Peg had put the Coleman lantern on and I felt relieved moving toward it, as my flashlight was just about out. My machine and I were totally covered with snow, but we made it!

Peg was shoveling snow...the storm was still with us. I fed the dogs, cut a mess of wood and went in and felt quite cozy with my wife, our animals, and all the provisions we have stored for the winter.

Dec.. 28: I awoke this morning...it was snowing. We now have a total of 30 new inches, or some five feet of snow. We figured about 10 feet had fallen since September. Tried to open the ranch trail with the snowmobile but got stuck...Peg put on her snowshoes and walked in front, breaking new trail. By dark we finally got through to the main trail. We dug ourselves out around the bunk house and settled in at dark for a hot supper, tired after a good day's work.

Dec.. 29: (My Dad's birthday.) Still snowing...42 inches of new snow in the last three days! With snowshoes on we still sink in past our knees but the snowshoes make it a lot easier getting around. As I looked out after supper, it was still snowing hard.

Dec.. 30: Six to seven feet of snow on the ground. Peg and I shoveled and then I broke our trails out again.

Dec.. 31: 16 degrees below zero this morning, but clear! Went up to the Hot Springs and shoveled snow. Some tourists came in by snowmobile. Got back to ranch at dark. Tonight, New Year's Eve! Peg and I ate supper, ate nuts and had ice cream sundaes, read a little, then went to bed at 11 p.m.

●●●

Peggy's diary—Dec. 27: I went out to shovel snow. No sooner had I started than I realized this was the biggest snowfall of the winter. I shoveled the light powder stuff and it seemed endless—thought it was nearly hopeless. But I kept up for several hours 'till I began to make some progress. I got half the paths cleared before dark, then continued after dark to the old outhouse...I was so tired with each shovel!

Gap was still not back and it was dark! The snow was coming down about an inch an hour, already about 15 inches by dark. Finally...I heard the snow machine and Gap was back. He'd had trouble but he had made it. At dinner, we sat down with a cozy feeling, knowing we were safe and warm...such a pleasant feeling—onto sleep and tomorrow to shovel again.

Dec.. 28-29: Yesterday's novelty became today's chore. It kept coming down all day and I recalled a few weeks earlier how I'd lamented the lack of snow to date. I guess it was not too late to repent my words.

During the next few days a pattern developed. We would snowshoe enough on the light powder that we could get the snowmobile over it. One of the most difficult chores was hauling water from the creek, a thing Gap had to do every Monday to keep us supplied. My job during this period was to reopen the trail to the road while we could still find it. On Dec. 29, I had to keep looking just to find the road marker and uncover it so we would know where trail met road.

I met two people on a snow machine trying to break trail. They were from the USFS. We had a cup of coffee, then they and Gap left to open the rest of the trail to the Springs. One man's machine even had a reverse on it! After I got a roast on to cook for dinner, guess I'll continue the shoveling. And if time allows, which I doubt, I'll try out the skis. Snow stopped falling but now drifting began. Clearing tonight and temperatures dropping fast.

Dec. 31: The last day of the year is going to be a beautiful one. Later, the frost clouds or fog came so heavy that it was clear and sunny that it was clear and sunny after all. This afternoon, I tried out the skiing. Crazy! Sure feel awkward. Like a baby learning to walk. Will take some work to get used to the wooden skis that Dr. MacLeod gave us. But I think it will make things easier travel on foot when one gets used to it. Temperature is dropping fast tonight. Will probably be the coldest night of the winter so far. It's New Year's Eve now—the quietest one yet.

•••

Gap—Jan. 1, 1974: Happy New Year! 34 below zero. Inside, 38 above, a bit cold. Got both wood stoves going. This 34 below reminds me of the 20 months I spent in Alaska. Coldest temp it ever got when I was in Alaska was 62 below zero. Peggy had never experienced anything like that.

The fact wasn't lost on me that both Peggy's well being and mine right now depended on heat, pure and simple. Well, I've got to split plenty of wood this morning, get the animals fed...had a good supper of lasagna and elk meat, salad, and home-made pumpkin pie. Peg had worked hard on a wonderful supper. It was a very clear, cold day and beautiful night.

Jan. 2: At 8 a.m. 44 below. Inside, 35 above. Fog. Cut wood aplenty.

Did I make any New Year's resolutions? Peg and I didn't

discuss them. Maybe later. Right now, my goal was to keep us and our brood of critters alive and comfortable.

•••

Peggy—Jan. 1, 1974: I spent the day inside making pies and lasagna for a special New Year's treat. At 35 below outside, I moved my 40-year-old cactus upstairs today...to save its life. The dogs even acted like they noticed the cold today—on their feet a lot. Gap put more straw in the ducks' boxes to keep them warmer. It was hard to get up this morning. It took courage to get out of bed to start the fire up again. It is surely helpful to have two wood stoves.

Jan. 2: Man, it was cold last night! We each got up at different times to keep the fire going but the room still dropped to 38 degrees inside.

We began to realize now the depth of our commitment. It would have been warmer indeed in Philadelphia or Salt Lake City. But we'll make it.

•••

Gap: Early in January, we began to see much more coyote activity around the bunk house. Apparently, the weather was causing even those hardy animals more difficulty in coping with the cold and in keeping their energy levels up. My entry for Jan. 5, reads: Saw two coyotes near Granite Falls today, so beautiful and wild; they belong here, fierce and roaming. What an animal to be able to survive the snow and cold! I took movies of them. Exciting!

Went up to the Hot Springs and saw that three skiers had used the pool, moved a large bench and did not deposit their dollar to swim in the container provided, so I began to track them down through the snow. I caught them halfway to the highway, five miles from the pool. They paid their money to me and said they were from upper New York State on vacation; they were very tired.

Peg got up early and continued crocheting on her table cloth she's making.

Jan. 8: About two miles from the ranch [bunk house] I noticed a hole about 6-7 feet deep and bits of hair and fur scattered around. At first, I thought a coyote had dug out a badger and there has been a terrible fight as badgers are tough and it would take at least two coyotes to kill a badger. As it turned out, two coyotes had dug the hole six feet deep down to an elk head discarded by hunters...imagine the scenting sense of those coyotes!

There were also coyote tracks near the ranch and a deep hole dug there by coyotes. They are getting very hungry now. I don't know what they were after but they are quite adept at digging out mice and rodents.

Jan. 9: Tried calling two coyotes with my wounded rabbit call but none came in. Later, just below the main ranch buildings, I saw two coyotes hunting for food, got some pictures at a distance. They then headed back into timber and out of sight.

THE COYOTES MOVE IN

Peggy—Jan. 2: 44 degrees below zero! Man it was cold last night. We each got up at different times to keep the fire going.

Jan. 3: The sky clouded and it warmed up. It only got to 5 below. Would like to go out on the skis again and start a leather project, but does not seem to be enough hours of the day. Everything one does takes so much more time here, with carrying water, chopping and carrying wood so much. Makes it hard to have that extra time which people think we have so much of here. It isn't quite like that!

Gap was excited this evening because he finally got to see two coyotes this afternoon—and film them. Said they were sure beautiful.

Al brought the mail today—a treat of course. Spent the afternoon doing laundry and hanging it up on the line upstairs that Gap put up yesterday. Reached completion of the fifth row on my crocheted tablecloth tonight, a quarter-way milestone. Ha! Maybe it won't take 20 years after all, just five.

Jan. 7: I finally got myself up earlier this morning. It is so hard to get out of a warm cozy bed in winter when it's black outside and cold inside too. The fire's out or almost...must wash the swim suits and towels (on the hand washboard) from the Hot Springs before they run out. Saves a tedious trip to town. I have come to rather mildly dread going to town anymore. Not that going to town isn't fun but all that getting ready, bundling up, waiting at the highway while Gap has to hitchhike to Roy Fisk's some 10 miles to get the ranch truck, then trying to pack all on the sleigh for the return trip and get back to a cold, cold bunkhouse which then takes hours and hours to heat up again.

Jan. 8: Good morning dear world. What a beautiful day. Must be going to dawn about 8:40 a.m. now that it is Mountain Daylight Time again. Arose early this morning to an intense light coming through the window—bright moonlight. Minutes later the moon went over the mountain and the sky was clear and the stars twinkling above the moonlight still shining on Open Door Mountain and the Dinosaur Peaks, at 10,000 feet elevation, way above the valley floor.

Went skiing during this time but fell and had to dig myself out of powder which was cold on the face. Some skier. After practice I began to be satisfied that I could get around the ranch reasonably well. Stoney, our dog disappeared during this time and Gap looked all over for him. Did the coyotes get him? We finally found him in the barn upstairs. He had climbed the stair ladder into the loft and then couldn't get back down, or was scared to. Gap got him down.

We were afraid to let him down after dark. The coyotes might attack. We had begun to find many coyote tracks moving very close to the bunk house at night. They must be starving!

On Jan. 11 we had an experience which could have been disastrous. I happened to go upstairs to get something when I noticed smoke gathered against the ceiling. The stove pipes upstairs where they were supposed to go out against the roof had slipped and tilted beneath the roof—aiming heat, soot and fire right against the rafters. They were charred and smoldering. It was already 5 p.m. and light was fading.

We turned off the stove draft downstairs, got ladder and tools, baling wire etc. and Gap managed to get the pipes back through the proper hole in the roof and fastened down with the wire. Amazing this had not happened sooner. What if it had happened while we were gone? Had someone above not been looking after us, it could have been disastrous.

•••

Gap: When I got back to the ranch near dark, Peg called me

excitedly. And as I went inside, I saw smoke coming from the roof. I could see where the smokestack had dropped from the hole in the ceiling and was burning the boards. Peg and I tightened the stack by using baling wire. We caught this just in time. Someone's looking out for us, I believe.

If the stack had come out earlier in the day it might have been even more precarious, since I don't usually come home until dark and it required both Peg and me to get the smokestack back in place. We will have to keep very close watch on problems like this in the future.

It could be said that we took on more adventure in moving to Granite Creek Ranch than we originally bargained. But it didn't seem to dim Peg's spirits for the frontier lifestyle we'd chosen. We just have to be careful.

Keep getting stuck in the snowmobile going to the Hot Springs. I get back at dark hungry and tired. Heard the thunderous roar of avalanches close by recently...lots of coyote tracks around the ranch. Larry brought us milk, ice cream and fruit whenever he could. Fun working with Larry. Had to keep clearing snow off the bunk house roof, about six feet in January, or the roof might cave in. Temperatures rose all the way to 40 above on Jan. 16. Saw a white weasel [ermine]. Heard on the radio that three men were killed in an avalanche in the Grand Tetons just north of here yesterday. Cut up the hind quarters of Larry's young horse he had to destroy...got 20 lbs. of stew meat for us, the dogs and birds.

Despite all that is said about eating horses as a last resort, the colt meat tasted good to us. Maybe we are just grateful for every blessing.

During this time, the coyotes kept howling at night and coming in very close to the ranch.

Jan. 21-29: The coyotes came in about 50 feet from the cabin in search of food this morning. They dug a hole very close to the bunk house. Peg baked a cherry pie yesterday. We had horse meat stew last night for supper. Very good! Peg is baking bread today. Had some folks at the Hot Springs today. They saw moose on their way up. Ten inches of new snow yesterday. Peg and I saw two coyotes hunting close to the ranch. Shoveled snow and cut wood.

Jan. 30-Feb. 8: Our power went out at 6 p.m! A friend, Roger, skied in to spend the night with us, brought vegetables, swam in the Springs and was to report to town that our power was out. We tried to reach the Springs the next day but too much snow to get through, had to turn back. Our power for the two light bulbs came back about 3:30 p.m. the next day after Roger reported it in town.

We got a note from Dr. MacLeod that Glen Exum, the mountain climber who had climbed Grand Teton more than any other man, some 300 times, is coming in to spend a few days with us; he is bringing a few friends along. He is now about 68. He also runs a mountain climbing school at Moose, north of Jackson.

Larry told us that Mr. and Mrs. Erwin Bauer, the famous wildlife photographer/writer will be coming in to stay with us to do a story on winter activities at Granite Canyon.

Peg dyed her leather goods today.

Coyotes have been howling this cold, clear morning. I cut wood and saw coyote.

Larry came near noon by snowmobile and brought Mrs. Ann Volk, a member of the DuPont family from Delaware. They had lunch with us, then left for Jackson.

Put some elk, moose and deer horns up on our buildings. Peg made cookies. Had moose roast for supper.

Put out some dog food for the coyote who seemed to be having trouble finding food. We were aware this would bring in more coyotes but we are not worried by their presence as long as the dogs and ducks are safely in their cages at night. We like seeing coyotes whenever possible. They are wild and belong here. Besides, there is nothing worse than starvation, for man or beast.

During this time the Colorado Springs Snowmobile Club came in to use the Hot Springs, 20 miles to the highway back and forth.

Saw the same cow elk that was with us at Granite in December. She was lying down along the Hoback River and looking a little thin. We got good pictures of her. Saw six moose. Took a sleigh ride with Larry through the National Elk Refuge; saw plenty of bull elk.

There are about 8,000 elk being fed nearby. They are a different animal this time of year, letting us ride out among them when they are so desperately hungry. I never knew an animal so hard to find when they are being hunted but different now. Even then, we're told they would stampede if anyone got out of the sleigh. Larry said two men saw three mountain lions on the refuge.

Feb. 15-30: The dogs and ducks are fine. Three cross country skiers broke into the pool concession building. I tracked and caught them at Little Granite and got their names and addresses. I went to the highway and got to the Roy Fisk Ranch and made a phone call to Jim Mauer, district forest ranger and reported the incident.

Heard coyotes again at night. Call of the Wild.

Quite a few tourists came to the Springs today. On trip to town saw hundreds of deer and elk along the Hoback. Wrote a sympathy card to my childhood friend, Dante Saldutti, whose father had died a few weeks ago. He was a very fine cobbler in our Italian neighborhood where I grew up. Dante and I went to school together and played sports. Feb. 28 temperatures went up to 52 degrees, warmest since the Fall. Had a group of boys on survival mission from Riverton, Wyo. come to the Springs. One boy was a full blood Indian. They had a good time in the snow.

March 1-5: Put up archery target on bales of hay and plywood. Saw a large beaver plowing through the snow.

 On Sunday morning, we listened to the Mormon Tabernacle

Choir from Temple Square in Salt Lake City, Utah from an Idaho station. This afternoon a coyote came in to feed on the sheepskins that are hanging on the fence. Crawled on my hands and knees and got pretty close for some movie pictures. Near dark, another coyote came in to join the first. It's been a long winter for survival. Any creature which can survive the long winter up here has my respect.

In the last few days we have noticed two species of birds, an Oregon junco and we think, a titmouse.

March 6, 1974: Our anniversary! Have been married nine years today. Celebrated the day shoveling snow and breaking trail. Peg helped shovel; then we went into the house and made pizza for supper. It was good!

March 7-20: Snowed another 12 to 15 inches. Never had snow like this ever, even in Alaska. Magazine photographers came to Springs to do a story of our area. We have not gotten to the highway for mail in about three weeks...The Mormon Church brought young girls for an overnight stay at the Hot Springs. They dug snow caves to sleep in. They came in on snowmobiles and a Big Cat, like a bulldozer which can go anywhere. About 9:45 we got word one of the girls had broken a leg playing with the snowmobile. We informed them we had no radio contact with the outside world.

We were later told they took her to a hospital in Jackson. We didn't hear from them again about her condition. Maybe we can report on this later.

Two snowmobiles came by and I jumped on my machine to catch up with them, hit a bad hole and I got bucked off the machine which continued on down the trail without a driver. I was made sore by the fall but not injured. I finally caught up with the other snowmobiles. They were from Pinedale and everything was OK.

On the way back, I came across what looked like lynx tracks. I began to follow and got down in a deep draw and got stuck pretty bad. Finally got out toward dark. Was wet and snowy when returning to the ranch. I watched for a moose that was in bad shape yesterday evening. Some wild ducks came into Granite Creek.

Shot some arrows at my target.

Twenty-four inches of new snow. Took us all day to shovel and break trails. Came upon some local people at the Springs who said they came through an avalanche in Hoback Canyon. It took them about three hours to shovel through. It rained today, the first since October.

We ate Peggy's baked rolls for supper while the coyotes sang.

•••

Peggy— Jan. 13: Ice on the roof edges, from icicles building up, has finally caused water to seep through several places in the bunk house. It does not drip in the room (yet) but it runs steadily down the logs of the wall. One night a week ago water came through the upstairs floor from somewhere in such force that it poured suddenly through the air while we were asleep and perfectly aimed itself... between the bed and dresser, my own head being only inches away. What a surprise that would have been right in my face! It stopped a minute, and that was all. Wonder when it will happen again?

Jan. 15-March 5: Heard avalanches. If only we could be a visual witness of these avalanches. How exciting! The forces of nature!

Forty degrees this afternoon. Feels like springtime.

We went to town and saw many wintering game animals in Hoback Canyon, including a herd of lovely deer against the turquoise skyline...a moose here and there too. It is just unbelievable and delightful...afterward it began to snow...the end of our Spring Fever for awhile.

Gap brought a middle-aged couple back to the cabin yesterday afternoon for coffee and conversation. They were independent commercial fishermen. Their home is near Easton, Mass. But their fishing operations take place off the California coast. They were vacationing in their off-season. They fish for swordfish, still using the harpooning technique. Would be interesting to watch.

I set out on the snowshoes for a time on a "mission of mercy" to take a bag of peanuts in the shell and sunflower seeds to the place around the clump of trees for the squirrels and birds. There were very few tracks. I hope they find the food and it will help them.

Gap just left to go the pool as a large group of snow machines had gone up a little earlier. I noticed out the window that he is stuck in the snow on the "water trail." This heavy, wet snow is a mess that always creates problems. I wonder what spring will bring—and how many more problems and backaches before the snow leaves and travel returns to wheeled vehicles?

Still it is heavy overcast. It seems a long time since we have seen the sun. Yesterday, I finally completed the scenic leather picture (with bears)...it is nearly ready for framing.... We cleaned the hot pool. I took a dip while Gap built a fire in the Concession Building stove. I washed and set my hair. How refreshed I feel now!

The pool was so hot that I didn't even feel the cold air after getting out. Some even like to roll in the snow between plunges in the pool. But this is only for the very hardy.

March 6: Our 9th anniversary. We awoke this morning to another whiteout. It had apparently snowed all night. So, how will we spend our anniversary? Shoveling snow.

SIGNS OF SPRING—WE THINK

Gap's Diary—March 18: I met a local trapper. I gave him a lift on my snow machine up to Little Granite Creek about three miles. He told me he's been trapping pine marten, beaver and fox. He said coyotes are too smart to catch and has not caught one coyote. He told me he saw a wolf last year in our area; a friend of his also saw this wolf in nearby Poison Creek.

This was somewhat shocking news, for the state of Wyoming and all others save for Minnesota near the Canadian border, and possibly northern Montana, have thought the timber or gray wolf extinct for years. The bounty on their heads placed by stockmen pretty well killed them off even in and around Yellowstone Park. It was exciting to hear there might be wolves in this region!

The trapper also said he had seen two dead elk this winter but didn't know why they were dead. He gave me 40 lbs. of frozen fish. I will use it as bear bait this spring.

March 19: Today is our shepherd dog's 12th birthday, pretty

old for a large dog. Stoney, our basset hound, was eight on March 12...heard the coyotes howling again close to the ranch this evening.

March 22: I cut Peggy's hair this morning. This evening we listened to the Lone Ranger on the radio. After dark is the only time we get any radio reception.

March 23-April 6: In the afternoon several dog sled teams came up to camp overnight. They were training their dogs, which are the husky breed and well trained to pull sleds. Peg's cousin, Larry, who is going to college in Utah, surprised us and skied in to spend a couple of days with us.

Saw a coyote sleeping in the snow. Don't see that every day. Saw the trapper and took him to Little Granite on my sleigh. He said he saw a pack of coyotes trying to get a young elk. He shot at but missed them with his handgun. Although I liked them around and didn't shoot them, coyotes are considered predators in Wyoming and can be shot on sight.

Tried to pull Peg up to the Hot Springs but too much snow for the machine and sleigh. Turned back. March may be called a "spring month" by some but it just keeps snowing. I measured 70 inches of packed snow—on level ground!

April 7, Palm Sunday: Talked to a cross-country skier who told me he had seen a bald eagle killing a duck!

April 9-13: Saw an airplane in the snow that had to make a crash landing because he lost his propeller up the canyon above the Springs. I talked to the pilot who said he was working for the Wyoming Game and Fish Dept. and was flying low to count bighorn sheep...he said none had wintered on the wind-swept ridges this year because of the snows we had. He did see sheep in other areas close by. They had to take the plane apart and get it out with snowmobiles, as he could not fly it. I helped them unload a wing, piece by piece, near the highway.

I've since thought how dangerous it is for those who work in this area and how lucky that pilot was.

Went to visit Jim Mauer and he showed me his Boone-Crockett mountain lion head he shot in Utah. Jim and I are planning a mountain lion hunt for next winter.... Snow was heavy and turned over the snowmobile in a snow bank on the way in. Didn't get in until 8:30 p.m. Heard a great horned owl on the way in.

Coyotes stole the dog's bone last night.

April 14, Easter Sunday: A bright, beautiful clear morning. Peg had made Italian cookies on the wood stove!

April 18-May 6: Snow is melting fast. Temperatures are up to 58 degrees. Got a newspaper clipping from my mother and father telling that Dr. Steinbach, the veterinarian that I worked for in Pennsylvania, had died. He taught me a lot about animals. I have many good memories of the days I worked for him, taking care of the horses and other jobs. He will be missed by all, a very fine vet, and extremely dedicated to his profession.

I went fishing in Granite Creek and caught 10 trout, six cut-throats and four brook trout. Had a good supper of trout, pota-toes, fresh dandelions I picked near the Hot Springs. A meal fit for a king—a gift of God!

Went fishing but caught only two trout. They just wouldn't bite today. Peg finished her large table cloth she's been working on for the last year. It's beautiful!

I called to the coyotes and they answered me this morning. On the way back from the highway a moose came off the mountain and nearly ran over me! Brought back strawberries, ice cream and milk. Saw 20 bighorn sheep.

Professional movie makers came into the Springs, including a man by the name of Dick Robertson who made the film *Brother of the Wind*, and the TV series of *Wild Kingdom*. He is now filming a story about Grizzly Adams, the Mountain Man. Robertson wants to do a scene in which he will roll over the falls [Granite Falls] into the pool below, so he told me. He says he raises other animals like wolves, lions, and bears. He said he might need my help.

Was supposed to meet Larry at the highway but my snow-mobile broke down and I had to walk nine miles on snowshoes. It took me 2 ½ hours. Saw six coyotes and howled to them and they howled back. Spent the night at Larry and Janet's home in Jackson.

I decided it was spring during this time as the Hoback River was swollen with snow melt. Also saw some robins. Spring is just in time. I saw two moose during this period and they were thin. Winter has been rough on them. Getting ready for my bear hunt... set up a 100-yard target and sighted in my 30-06. Will be going out after bear soon! Saw two bears on May 5.

Spring is here. The trail is very bad. Difficult to pull the sleigh even when we can get through with the snow machine.

During this time Peggy recorded in her diary that she heard the roar of an avalanche at one time and witnessed snow pouring over a high cliff on Terrace Mountain. "As it cascaded over and crashed on the ledges below, it created a rumble and a billow of snow clouds mushrooming up from where it was landing. The ripple effect could be seen in white puffs all the way down the canyon. It was surely an exciting and beautiful spectacle!"

•••

Peggy: The great fracture of melting snow on the other side of the canyon is moving farther downhill day by day. We've been watching it for several weeks and recently it is moving much faster. After the last snow we had, it moved at least 200 feet in one night. Altogether, it has slipped down the mountain at least 100-120 feet so far.

When the LDS [Latter-day Saints, Mormons] girls came up to the Springs to camp, it was a day of fun, a day of delight. I enjoyed browsing and chatting. The LDS girls are a fine bunch and had such a good time on their outing. By coincidence, another church group came up too, from the Pinedale Baptist Church. But by 3 p.m. there was no one there but Gap and me. We went for a long swim and enjoyed feeding crumbs to the little mountain chickadees which live near the pool.

Thursday will be the anniversary of the actual beginning day of our move. It seems a million years ago! (And about was.)

One year ago today we drove out of our Pennsylvania farm home and began a long journey clear across the country...in a two-truck caravan. It seemed a very worrisome trip at the time—and rather was. So glad it is over and done!

How time and miles do fly in our lives here on Earth!

The water in the Springs is very hot now. [It gets hotter when everything freezes up and no snowmelt runs into the springs.] The water makes you so relaxed it weakens you.

During this time I enjoyed many walks in the woods, feeding sunflower seeds to the birds and squirrels. When Brave, our large white German shepherd, followed me on snowshoes I noted he walked directly behind me. If I stopped, he wouldn't go ahead. He is smart enough to let me break trail and then he gets along very well. I saw grouse in the trees. One day I saw an ermine [weasel in winter coat]. The woods are full of life in spite of the snow.

March 19: The snow finally melted enough off the roof that

water no longer ran down inside of the bunk house walls. That was getting to be a tiresome nuisance. I hope it does not come back.

In the meantime, it has snowed enough that it is difficult in the combination of melting snow and mud to get to town and take care of laundry and buy things we need like vegetables and fruit.

It was even more difficult to get around on skis and on one occasion after Larry started out, we could see it was going to be a particularly nasty day, so Gap got the snowmobile/sleigh and gave them a lift to the highway. It wasn't easy even then but better than skiing the entire 10 miles.

During this time I watched a coyote lying on the woodpile. He would lift his head to look around, then tuck it under his tail. I tried to get its attention by calling, whistling and "whining" like a distressed animal but it didn't pay any attention. Finally, it got up and walked away, stopping to stare at me now and then.

March 28-April 9: Heavily snowing. Now and then the wind and snow becomes very intense and gusty, sucking the bunk house door right open.

Snow, snow, snow...seems to never stop. Not that we are that tired of snow, but we crave sunshine and blue skies. Awoke again to heavily falling snow, just as all day yesterday. The month of March came in with storms and looks like it will go out the same. What happened to the lamb?

I said to Gap that at least in March we hadn't lost our electricity and 30 minutes later, I was washing dishes by candlelight and Coleman lantern. Must keep my mouth shut. Fortunately, it didn't last long this time.

After going to town one day, we arrived at the trailhead for the 10-mile snowmobile trip to the bunk house at 6 p.m. We couldn't carry all our load in one trip and left the laundry (19 batches) at the trailhead to bring in the next day. (Of course, it was frozen when we returned Saturday morning.) But on the way in, the moon was beautiful that night. It loomed before us full on the top of the mountain ridge facing us. I always enjoyed the view of the mountains in the distance as we took this trip—noting how different the features appeared from far off than from nearby at the ranch. We could not quite make the hill in one place with the sleigh, so I walked part of the way by light of the moon.

We had a surprise this morning when we were on our way to Hot Springs. We reached the bridge to find it collapsed sometime in the night or early morning. There it all lay in a heap down in the stream. Guess the snow weight was finally too much for it. So, for a couple of months it will be a long way around by way of the lower bridge.

April 10: I wondered if Gap would attempt to return 38 miles from town in the storm. About 8 p.m. he arrived snow-covered and bringing more fruits and vegetables...and a surprise for me...a lovely large bunch of Easter daffodils (and somehow not at all damaged). What a breath of spring...yellow daffodils. I hope they last long.

Partly sunny and warm today. Yeah! Yeah!

I spent the day as the Easter Bunny making goodies and dipping chocolate cocoanut Easter eggs, baking traditional Italian cookies and making dinner preparations for Sunday.

Easter: We arose to a gorgeous day, one befitting Easter itself... the glory of the sun shone from each mountain peak. All was still and the sun brilliant as it came over the mountains, casting down its warm rays through the crisp morning air.

April 15-30: I went for a lovely, quiet walk about 6 p.m. The beauty of these days has made me realize how lucky we are to have such an experience as this.

Another gorgeous day! I set off for an afternoon snowshoe hike. I did something I'd wanted to do for weeks: walk along the east side of Granite Creek to the Falls, passing all the beautiful springs. I found four hot sulphur springs below the falls...and what a delight, I found the first patch of green grass and blooming dandelions.

At the Hot Springs there is much bare ground. Delightful too, the clusters of yellow buttercup-like flowers.

This day dawned even more beautiful than the others. It was too exquisite a day to waste indoors, so I decided to enjoy it. I rode to the pool with Gap in the sleigh, bracing his snowshoes, fishing pole and creel. He went off to fish in the beaver ponds below the Falls while I remained at the pool. I took a few pictures, close ups of buttercups...then went for a swim and laid on the deck working on a leather carving design. Crocheted a little and swam some more. What a Heaven! What more could one ask for?

Opposite page, top: Gap in Alaska, 1958, as a member of the U.S. Mountain Troops. Bottom: Gap's father traveled from Pennsylvania to visit Gap and Peg. He is pictured here riding Sunny Jim. Gap's father cultivated his son's love of the great outdoors.

Slim Bassett, pictured above, homesteaded on Granite Creek and was a good friend of Granite Creek Ranch owner Dr. Don MacLeod. Gap met Slim when Slim was in his 80s, and recalls that he was a top outfitting hand and hunting guide for many years. Slim told Gap he killed the last wolf in Granite Creek in 1929.

70

THE EARLY GRANITE YEARS

This page, top: Dr. Don MacLeod unpacking elk off a pack horse at Granite Ranch. Bottom: "Doc" with his Irish setter, Mac. Opposite page, top: Doc with Andy, his two-year-old mule. Bottom: Shane and Laura Moore, Doc's grandchildren, and Gap display a fine string of fish caught in the Gros Ventre Wilderness. One of Doc's favorite places was a small, stocked lake nestled beneath Corner Peak that today bears his name. Dr. MacLeod was one of Jackson Hole's early doctors and was much beloved. Before securing his own hunt camp, Gap worked for Granite Creek Ranch as a hunting guide and packer.

Top and opposite page: Louie Hansen worked summers at Jackson Mercantile in downtown Jackson. Autumn and winter, he trapped the high country in Crystal and Jagg Creek drainages. He was found dead, sitting against a post near Granite Ranch, in the early 1940s. Gap came across Hansen's old cabins up Crystal Creek and Jagg Creek. On one, a frying pan was still attached to the log wall.

Bottom: Gap saddles a horse in front of the Granite Creek Ranch bunkhouse.

Top: Gap transports wood via snowmobile to Granite Creek bunkhouse. Transporting and chopping wood, pictured below, was a constant chore to keep the poorly insulated structure warm. Gap and Peg were the first people to winter at Granite Hot Springs, constructed by a CCC crew in the 1930s.

Top: Gap and Larry Moore, Doc MacLeod's son-in-law, shovel snow off the roof of the Granite Creek Ranch bunkhouse to keep it from collapsing. Bottom: The outhouse that Gap and Peg used at Granite Creek Ranch. The bunkhouse had no running water. It had to be hauled in five gallon milk cans from nearby Granite Creek.

Top: Gap poses near The Kristie Cat, an over-snow machine that, in theory, should have made life easier, but in reality often broke down. Bottom: Peggy enjoys a ski alongside Stoney, the Pucci's basset hound, at Granite Ranch.

Opposite page, top: Heavy snows nearly bury Peg and Gap's cabin at Granite Hot Springs following a heavy snowstorm. Bottom: Gap enjoys a moment with a sled dog team up Granite Creek.

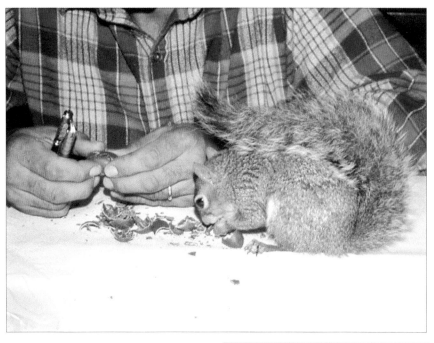

Top: Peg's pet squirrel Butchy and Gap share nuts together. Butchy kept Peg company when Gap was gone on extended trips or chores. Bottom: Peg enjoys the snow on a warm, early spring day—demonstrating that life at the hot springs was not all work, all the time.

SIGNS OF SUMMER

———

Peggy: As the snow began to recede, I decided there was some benefit to the white stuff. I went out with my camera to see if I could find tracks of unusual animals. By the bridge, I came upon a set of tracks which fascinated me. My diary records that..."they were too large for coyote tracks. Stride is too long. The books points to wolf or lynx. I followed them: the famous beaver ponds featured in *National Geographic*, May, 1974. After reading about them, I wanted to see for myself. The tracks went right to the ponds, where I finally left them.

I wasn't certain how far they would go, so I remained to inspect the ponds. The beaver ponds were just as written—and fascinating, too. As I approached, there were ducks everywhere and a pair of sandhill cranes. As they saw me, the cranes made a lot of racket before they flew, alerting everything. The ducks moved farther away. There were tracks of a cow and calf moose all around. I sat under a tree and watched the beaver house, hoping to see the beavers. I saw them swimming fast in the water, but didn't get a good look. As I finally arose, the ducks flew all over.

As I walked home, it was interesting to see the "diary in the snow," all the tracks and signs winter has preserved. Snow melts and falls again and the tracks were here all over again. It is very interesting to observe the reappearance of the story of winter. But before long, the snow will be gone...will I miss it?

•••

Gap's diary—May 7-11: Heading back to the ranch, we had a hard time for the first four miles. Peg walked most of the distance. I pulled the sleigh with the supplies across bare ground. Finally, we hit snow and made it home about 8:30 p.m.

Had a hard time hauling water. Got my pack board ready for my bear hunt. Saw one bear around supper time on steep slope across west side of the bunk house on south exposure. Will try to get him tomorrow—or him get me!

Went bear hunting where I'd seen the bear. Had a 30-06 and .44 Mag. handgun. Started out with snowshoes, got too steep, left the shoes and then continued up the slope. Never did see the bear up to about 8,000 feet. Got back to ranch about dark.

Went trout fishing at the beaver ponds and had no luck. Trout have disappeared. Don't know where they go this time of year with the high fast water but they are not to be seen. Saw some wild ducks. Went bear hunting in the afternoon, climbed south side slope to watch for bears. Saw four moose, no bears!

May 12: Today is Mother's Day! I called my folks when we were at Margaret Feuz' home in town. They seemed fine, although Dad has a cyst removed from his throat, is on leave from work for awhile.

Carried 50 lbs. of fish on my back up bare south slope (less snow attracts bears) for bait. Hung it from tree in burlap bag. Later in the afternoon, I took my rifle and climbed south exposure of Open Door Mountain to look for bear, saw nothing but grouse.

Took Peg to the highway to get the truck. She is going to Salt Lake City to see her mother and bring some things back for us. She will be gone a week or so!

Larry came in to try and plow the road open heading to the ranch. I helped him; we got stuck!

May 15: Caught two young men who broke into the summer homes. Picked up their tracks at the Clymer cabin, saw glass on door broken. Had to go to Hoback Junction to phone the sheriff and head forest ranger, 38-mile trip. Still using snow machine half way down. Got back to the ranch at 10 p.m. Fixed my supper and went to bed about 1 a.m. Peg is still in Salt Lake City.

During this time the Forest Service came in to see what they could do to repair the bridge. Larry did some more plowing on the road. Opened up irrigation water for ranch use. I let the dogs and ducks out to enjoy being out and free. But I had to keep a watch out because after dark I talked to the coyotes!

May 18: Peg is still in Salt Lake City! Larry came up and finished plowing out the snow. For the first time this winter we can drive into the ranch. I dug a new hole for our outdoor toilet.

May 19-25: Helped Larry put up some barbed wire fence. We found some semi-precious jasper stones. Snowed on us all day and was very nasty.

Saw first deer of spring moving back into high country. Peg is still in Salt Lake City. So made supper for Larry and me.

Peggy came home today!

Got a letter that my Uncle Gaspari Pucci, Italian immigrant, had died at age 93 years old. I first started hunting on his farm in Pennsylvania when I was 10. I'll always remember him. We have the same name!

Peg and I have to walk to the Hot Springs The road is still snowed in but too much mud to use the snowmobile.

May 27, 1974: Memorial Day. Seeing moose about every day.

May 29: Rained all day. Caught two boys who broke into the concession stand.

June 1-5: Peg and I saw the first-born calf moose of the season today. Went bear hunting this evening. Saw moose and five deer. No bear. Climbed to about 9,000 feet.

Today is the first day we can drive the truck to the Hot Springs. Snow is about gone on trail. Met two young men charged by cow moose when they came across her dead calf. They had a narrow escape. Saw six antelope in Larry's fields.

During this time we were not allowed to get our hopes too high that summer had arrived, for it snowed all day June 7. We checked the Hot Springs and found someone has been fooling around with it. Finally, we found it vandalized; someone had stopped up the outlet and made a muddy mess that required two days to clean out. Found foul language graffiti on the sign. Yes, summer must be arriving, what with easier access. Are the hippies back again?

Meantime, I continued to go bear hunting to no avail. The dog killed a snowshoe rabbit. I didn't let it go to waste, cleaning it to eat later. We saw many more cow and calf moose and I took movie pictures of them while not getting too close.

While helping Larry round up his 50 horses, we had two of them run away. Driving the horses [by horse back] from Pinedale to Granite Ranch, a distance of some 60 miles, lasted two days. We were photographed by some movie photographers from Eastman Kodak who were making a film entitled *The American Cowboy*. It is for the U. S. Bicentennial, they said. Last of the old horse drives in Jackson Hole!

The sheriff's office said they would have someone to patrol the Hot Springs at night. They also got us a field radio to keep in contact with the sheriff and Forest Service.

When I got home one day I found our pet duck had died. We had raised her from a baby duckling. I buried her near Butch under the pine trees by the bunk house.

June 16-20: Had trouble at the Springs last night when three carloads, about 15-20 people, demanded to swim at midnight. I told them the pool closed at 8 p.m. [Signs all around gave the pool's open hours.] I called the sheriff's office on our new radio. The sheriff's officers came and we ran them off. These people were drinking with a 16-year-old girl in their company and littered the entire recreation area. They had also put up rocks blocking water and causing the pool to fill up with sediment. They were hollering and shouting and disturbing the peace. We warned them about returning after hours. We also took down their license plate numbers.

It took most of the next day to clean up the mess. Saw young bull moose near the pool. Had a good day!

The next day I caught four more people trying to get into the hot pool at midnight. I gave them a warning ticket. [It would be up to the Forest Service to give out citations which would hold up in court.]

Had some trouble today as some people wanted to swim nude and one individual used obscene language. Peg was upset and sent for me. I was at the ranch shoeing horses. I went out there and ran them out. Grabbed the long-haired trouble maker by the hair and stood him up. And ushered him out of the pool area.

I hired a young man today to help at the pool. He will be in our concession building and be a night watchman. Seems like a nice young man! Maybe I can get some sleep now. Mark chased eight people out of the Springs last night.

June 22-25: Peg went to town to help Margaret Feuz with her art show. Mark ran out more people at 2 a.m.

Last night the people from the Cowboy Bar came into the pool to cause trouble. I also ran out 10 other people who came in to swim after hours. Mark came down to tell me his car had been vandalized, coil wire and spark plugs cut. Distributor cap broken. I reported his about 12: p.m. Mark drove out three people at 1 a.m.

This was beginning to get very old. But there was much more to come.

SUMMER AT LAST

Gap's Diary: June or not, it continued to snow through early part of the month and temperatures often dropped below freezing. I cut wood not only for the winter supply but because we needed it right now, mornings and night. Mark had groups trying to get in the Springs after hours and Peggy was very busying accompanying the paying patrons in the daytime.

On June 29, I got word that one of this region's old cowboys, Bill Daniels, had died. He was cremated and his ashes scattered to the wind at Two Ocean Pass near Yellowstone. The ceremony was simple but beautiful at the Turner Ranch overlooking the mountains. My diary says, "He was last of the mountain men in this area and an old-time cowboy. "

July 1-10: Today I got up at 5 a.m. and started my first official day working for Larry. Rounded up horses in the morning and started working with some colts...the weather has been sunny and warm...worked with the horses today. Saw moose and deer as I wrangled horses this morning. Shod three horses today. [The dictionary definition of wrangler is "A ranch hand who takes care of the saddle horses." But it is more than that. Wranglers take care of saddle and pack horses daily, often dozens of them, turning all out to graze in evenings and bringing them back in early mornings. This itself is usually done by horseback.]

Peggy has been busy at the pool. Lots of campers in the campground. Granite Ranch had a cookout for supper tonight. Helped Larry get his horse-drawn wagons prepared today and we took a ride. Was Scott's birthday. Peg made it down for supper.

Doc MacLeod and I took some guests up Swift Creek Trail. Some beautiful country. Been busy taking people on trail rides. Once again, this means much work for wranglers. We must feed and saddle horses for the guests on their trail rides. Weather really nice. Getting dry finally!

July 11-20: Had to put back barrier post that someone knocked down last night. Doc MacLeod and I took guests to Shoal Creek for the day. Big, beautiful country; saw moose, deer, coyote.

Power went out at 2 a.m. this morning. Found trouble and repaired damage. Wrangled horses at 5:45 a.m. and had a good day. Had to be in the saddle every day by 6 a.m.

The Steinbachs took a whitewater trip today. We visited in the evening.

Early this morning the Steinbachs left Granite Canyon to go back east. I wrangled this morning, then went to Thayne and Afton to pick up the chaps that the Indian Big John made for me, and a set of saddle bags. Got home late.

July 25: Temperature 34 degrees this morning. Has been down to 30 degrees in July but soon warms up and gets sunny; lots of sunshine. Little rain. Cut wood with Larry, Doc and the boys. Peg went to town. She's been busy at the pool.

Aug. 4: Rode in last night after five days camped in the wilderness with Doc MacLeod and Don. We had two government men from the U.S. Bureau of Mines looking for mineral deposits and studying a proposed Gros Ventre Wilderness. We rode horses many miles, panned streams for mineral deposits. Saw moose, large herd of elk, caught trout. Still have five more days to guide these men around. Today went up to Gros Ventre Canyon to check on Slim and Grover Bassett's 18 mining claims, found his old camp at about 10,500 feet elevation, rise of 3,500 feet above Granite Ranch.

Aug. 8-20: Snowed on the higher peaks last night! Temperature this morning was 32 degrees. Snowed on peaks again!

Worked on saddles today. Larry took guests and floated the Snake River. I took guests over to Shoal Creek to fish. They got some nice ones. Saw moose.

Don saw a bear when we were wrangling horses this morning. I saw coyotes after I howled at them. Temp at 27 degrees this morn. Weather nice and sunny during day.

Temp at 27 again this morning. Peg and the Moores and I went to town to vote in a local election. Today I shod horses all day, have 39 head to do; about half done. My horseshoe training at Penn State pays off! Peg, Janet and kids went shopping in Idaho Falls. Saw bobcat this morning.

Aug. 21-31: Peg, Larry and kids and I went to MacLeod Lake today at elevation 10,500 feet. Fishing great; we caught 33 trout, 1 ½ - 2 lbs. apiece. Good day!

Dan Denahaye, the famous knife-maker, came to Granite Ranch to visit. I guided him. We went to MacLeod Lake, caught 16 nice trout. Dan really enjoyed his trip to the high country. I was given several of Dan's knives as a gift by him for his trip.

During this time we went sage grouse hunting and shot 23 grouse and flushed up about 150.

Sept. 1-9: We finished shoeing about 50 head of horses. Took the first string of pack horses nine miles to set up the hunting camp and some of the tents.

Peg came up to spend a few days. Saw two bull moose near camp, velvet hanging in shreds from all antlers, all bloody from rubbing the velvet off.

Weather has been sunny and warm, cold at nights. Today, Larry took the fishermen and Peg back to the ranch. Fishermen caught many trout. Buster Wilson, wrangler and part-time guide, and I will stay in camp. I took Buster to the Box Canyon for scouting where we will hunt the first day. Buster and I split wood all day. Heard the coyotes and a great horned owl during the night.

Got horses packed and led them back to the ranch for hunters' supplies. Met Tom along the trail bringing the first party of hunters and camp cook; Ruth Kerns is her name. Buster and I returned with supplies. Eighteen miles today with pack strings, which always slows things down.

Sept. 10: First day of elk season. We took out eight elk hunters. I lined up the horsemen for the first elk drive. We climbed the mountain in the dark. Later, I took a hunter with me and climbed near 10,000 feet looking for elk. We shot no elk today. One old-timer had a chance to shoot but could not locate the bull in his sights. I heard some bugle, as the bulls do when challenging each other to a fight. Got back at dark with my hunter.

Sept. 11: I chased out 10 large buck deer from high ledges. Hunters with me had no deer permits!

Sept. 12: Third day of elk season and still none of our hunting party has shot an elk. One fellow saw a moose today. I saw five elk today but no shooting! Larry chased some bulls and cow elk that he drove through but no one got a shot at them. Weather has turned cold; some light snow. I took my hunter to 9,500 feet today in search of elk.

Sept. 14-20: Our hunters shot two bull elk today after a rough hunt. One of our hunters wounded a big bull moose. After a long day of tracking, we got him. A hunter of mine bagged a trophy mule deer with antlers that went 30 inches wide. One hunter saw 11 elk but he got zero shots.

By this time, I was beginning to feel like we were doing well as several more hunters shot bull elk and a bull moose. I had been experimenting with an elk call, designed to challenge a herd bull to take away his harem of cows and lure him into running toward the bugle to fight it. This time in September is height of the elk rut in high country, so I was excited about the possibilities of calling in the big battlers.

I recorded this in my diary; for Sept. 27, 1974: "I bugled in a bull elk and my hunter missed two shots at it. The next day I called in another bull and my hunter fired 14 shots but missed them all.

While my clients didn't score, I felt they couldn't blame the guide.

As a hunting guide, I kept one thing in mind and that was being fair to the hunter. He/she selects an outfitter-guide carefully because the investment in time and money is huge and they want to make the very most of it. This hunt might be the one of a lifetime, a dream quest for trophy elk or deer that won't be equaled again. I want to make certain I give my hunters my very best, be ready, sharp, helpful, alert for his success.

When I first came to Jackson Hole, before moving there, I appreciated the way my outfitter met me at the airport and made me feel welcome to his allotted territory. He was very helpful in getting me into the game and I appreciated him going the extra mile for me.

But I also got a bad taste in my mouth. I downed a trophy buck antelope which I followed until dark. The next day I thought I knew right where it was. But another hunter had tagged it! There isn't always a lot the guides can do in a situation like that but they can try to make certain the hunters deal fairly with one another. They can look out for their clients and go to bat for them. I determined early in the process that it was a great honor and responsibility to be a hunting guide and I was going to try to live up to that lofty title.

One of my challenges, as with all guides in wild terrain, is search and rescue. I got my chance to help in early October when a woman and her son came to the ranch asking for help. The lady's husband had broken his leg and was lying somewhere on the mountain waiting for help! I recognized his name. He was the trapper from Jackson I'd met the past winter.

My diary reads: "The weather was cold and it was getting

dark and no one knew if he had matches to build a fire. He was alone. Dr. MacLeod's grandsons Scott, Shane, Buster, the trapper's teenage son and myself got a litter and went into the mountains to find him. We located him by my firing a pistol in the air. He only fired one shot but we found him. He did have a fire to warm his broken leg. We helped Dr. MacLeod put a splint on the leg, then we carried the trapper down a steep mountain. When we got to a dirt road, we loaded him in a pickup truck and took him to the hospital in Jackson 40 miles away. I got back to the ranch at 1 a.m.

After that, we didn't hear from the family for a time about how he was doing, but it appeared that with a cooperative effort, we had saved the man's life.

After that, we packed out all the tents from the high mountain camp and hunted out of the ranch. We also camped out on Dell Creek, high on a mountain. We saw 65 elk that evening but our hunter never got a shot! We lived part of this time on spruce grouse I shot with my pistol. They weren't as difficult to get in the sights as the elk. Slept on a steep mountain upon old elk beds to keep from rolling down the mountain.

In the middle of October, Dr. MacLeod found a wounded bull elk and guided one of our hunters to it and he took it. We brought in new hunters and game wardens came in to check everyone out. By Oct. 30, we had eight inches of snow on the ground. My hunters found and took some trophy deer. I packed out the deer on my saddle horse, walking the four miles to the ranch. I shot a five-point buck [western count] in a new area where few of us had been before. There is so much country here that there is always some exciting place to go.

By Nov. 10, all the hunters were gone and it was back to Peggy and me at the ranch with an occasional visit from Larry. It snowed all day and I realized the challenge of another winter was upon us. Were we better prepared than the last one? We hope so. We shall see.

BONDING

Before we settled completely into the winter routine at the bunk house, we took a trip eastward. First stop was the Black Hills in northeast corner of the state. Here, I hunted antelope and white-tail deer for several days. After stalking and crawling about a mile on my belly, I shot an antelope. They were very spooky as today (Nov. 7) was last day of the pronghorn season. I could hardly get near them and made a one-shot kill following my long stalk.

The next day, I went into the Black Hills forest to try for white-tail deer and turkey. Had one day to hunt. Shot a young buck deer, no turkey. Saw plenty of doe deer.

Peggy spent this time in our truck camper, a little shopping. Now, we headed for Kansas to visit her grandmother born on an Indian reservation in Oklahoma, plus aunts and uncles. Visited in Lawrence and Wichita. We spent a week there.

Nov. 27: Left for Pennsylvania for a visit with my parents and relatives. Thanksgiving Day we traveled all day and made it half-way through Ohio. Good weather so far.

We arrived in Pennsylvania, had lunch in our camper. It is still trying to snow; the clouds have been dark and stormy. Arrived that night at my folks' home. Glad to see them doing so well!

Dec. 28, 1974: Left Pennsylvania this morning after four weeks at my folks' home. Went deer hunting with my Dad while there, but the hunting was poor in Pa. Dad missed a doe on the last day.

Peg helped my Mom and Dad on the new home they bought. They are selling the home where we lived for the past 20 years or so. We also got to visit lots of relatives and friends, including our good friends, the Pitera family. My Grandmother fell and broke her hip; she is 86 years old and recuperating in a nursing home. She's looking better. My Uncle Morris had a heart attack and a light stroke while we were here in Pa. He seems to be coming along. He is 84 years old.

It is always raining in Pa. We had a nice Christmas, went to church after missing Mass for a long time. Had lots of good Italian food my Mother and Peg cooked. Saw people I haven't seen in years.

One more thing before I close for the day. It seems to me that the eastern half of the U.S. is becoming a large city. In the two years that Peg and I have moved away, we noticed extremely heavy traffic and city atmosphere in the area where we lived. In areas where I hunted as a boy, many new homes, condominiums, high rise apartments and shopping centers and businesses everywhere! Some of the people also seem to be "inner city types," high-strung, short-tempered, money-conscious, materialistic and in poor physical shape.

Dec.. 29: My Dad's birthday. He is 62 today.

We returned through Illinois and went to Peg's brother's home for a visit. All of Peg's family seem to be well. A snowstorm hit us in Iowa. We camped along U.S. 80 and headed for Wyoming again the next morning. Got across Nebraska by 8 p.m. We saw six deer.

Jan. 4, 1975: Got a late start this morning. Water froze in camper and had to thaw out before starting. Got into Wyoming...high winds and ground blizzard in the Medicine Bow National Forest. Camped for the night in the Red Desert.

Jan. 7: Peg and I with our supplies made it into Granite Ranch with snowmobiles and sleighs. Larry helped us also. Yesterday, Larry and I broke trail through a storm that dumped 24 inches of new snow at the ranch.

It was tough going and we got stuck quite a few times. I kept thinking: "Welcome Home."

Jan. 8: Woke up this morning to 15 inches of new snow. Broke trails around ranch and to our water hole at Granite Creek. Could not get to highway 10 miles away. Saw moose near bunk house. Peggy straightened things up there.

For the next few weeks, it was much the same as the first winter recorded in our 1974 diaries. Temperatures below zero. At times after returning from town it was 20 degrees indoors. I tried to keep shoveling paths through four feet of accumulated snow. We had our "Kristi" snow machine repaired and it holds four people. It has a roof on it with cat tracks like a bulldozer.

During this time our shepherd dog, Brave, who is 13 years old, got crippled up pretty bad in the hips. I started him on medication. Stoney, our basset hound, is doing fine. Our duck was killed by a bobcat at the hunting camp cook's home! (We had hauled our ducks there by snowmobile when we were away.) As before, we began seeing moose. Coyotes are howling near the bunk house. The coyotes and I, we keep talking to each other. The elk are returning to feed grounds near our home. Kristi snow machine broke down. Temps went way below zero. Repaired Kristi. It broke again. Snowed. Managed to fix Kristi at home.

Jan. 27-31: Temp dropped to 18 below. Kristi broke down again. Snowshoed 18 miles from ranch to nearest phone to call Larry to get it fixed. Talked with my friends, the coyotes. Split wood as I do every morning. Takes lots of wood to keep us warm.

Feb. 2: Groundhog Day. Snow stopped with a total of 10

new inches. Today, some bank employees had a picnic at the Hot Springs. These people were crude and unruly! They all entered the pool without paying. Their language was foul and out of line as this is a public pool and three or four other families were also bathing. Some of these people throw their garbage [chicken bones] into the pool area along with beer cans. I had to correct the situation by getting their attention...and put their garbage in filler bags provided for them. They drank too much. Other families told me they had to pick up their beer cans on the trail to the pool. I also saw beer cans on the trail as I headed home after dark. These bank people were very disappointing, as they were supposed to be educated and professional. Some of the other families were not very happy with them, as they seemed to take over the area. There were about 20 bank employees there.

Feb. 9: A new group came to the pool, drank too much, littered, used foul language. They drove their snowmobiles into a forbidden zone by the pool. They left empty wine bottles inside the pool! Seventy five per cent of them were stone drunk! One said he worked for the Forest Service. They gave me a hard day. The Forest Service employee, being drunk, dove into shallow water and split his head pretty bad. Caused bleeding!

I've often been asked why we didn't do more about arresting or punishing the people who came to the pool who didn't pay, littered etc. I guess I'm just patient. I just keep looking for the best in people. But I'm also wondering if I'm too optimistic.

During February, I thought it would never stop snowing...63 inches on the level ground. It snowed nine more inches after I took the measurement. I tried to break trail to the highway but had to turn back after two miles. We are now cut off from the world. We can't get out and they can't get in. Peg carved leather today.

Feb. 13: Twenty inches of new snow. Put out the frozen sheep entrails for the coyotes and pine martens. Heard on the radio that snow slides have blocked both the Snake and Hoback river canyons. I heard the rumble of avalanches today above the ranch. Breaking a trail to highway impossible.

Feb. 14: St. Valentine's Day. Ninety-three inches of snow. Peg and I managed to break a trail to the highway but snow was deep! We had to shovel much snow off the truck before we could head for Jackson. It was buried.

Feb. 15-30: Larry came and we shoveled snow off the ranch buildings. During this time a husband and wife on cross country skis came to our ranch. The husband was sick. They had seen our dim light and the wife helped her husband toward it. She was a nurse and thought her husband was having an appendicitis attack. He was in intense pain and we made him as comfortable as possible. We were much worried. The situation was desperate. Fortunately we were able to get radio reception with the Forest Service; they called the hospital and were able to get an ambulance to the highway. I got the man in a sleigh and covered him with blankets for the trip out. We arrived before noon and I bade him farewell as the ambulance took him away. At the hospital he had emergency surgery. When Walt and his wife returned to their home in Portland, Oregon, they sent us thanks!

Peggy and I bought some new property and a cabin in Hoback Canyon and we went over to take some measurements of the rooms. Had to snowshoe in. We also took some local newspaper people from Teton Village into the Hot Springs. They took pictures and will do a story for the paper. Had our first real paying guests of the year at the Springs; took them in by sleigh. Had a flat tire on Kristi. Heard strange wild animal roaring from the forest. Sounded like a mountain lion.

March 1-15: More people to Hot Springs but their snow machine broke down and they came to the ranch for help. We had a sleigh tour come in but Bill got the sleigh stuck in the deep snow. Kristi broke down again.

On March 6, Peg and I celebrated our 10th Wedding Anniversary. "Happy Anniversary!" we told each other. Then we celebrated by going to the window and watching the snow falling down. Two days before, we had gone to town over an avalanche on the trail, pulling the sleigh across by brute strength. The avalanche was 20 feet deep and 150 yards long. We had to cut a trail over it with a steel bar and shovel. It was the only way to get supplies through. Last few days were rough.

A Mormon youth group came into the Hot Springs and camped overnight. Went down to our new property on the Hoback to see some builders. Walked about four miles to the highway where the mailman picked me up. Larry welded some pieces on the Kristi for me. Pulled out a man who was stuck in the snow... used the Kristi. Shortly after that, the Kristi broke down again. Larry gave us a ride back to the ranch in his snowmobile. Parts for Kristi came through the mail so we repaired it and drove it back home. Put out sheep entrails for the coyotes. They are coming close to the bunk house to do their howling.

March 16-30: St. Patrick's Day, March 17. Peg baked bread all day. Peg has been having pains in her head the past few days. Neuralgia, some people call it. We are watching it day by day.

There have been seven elk trapped by deep snow that I've been feeding all winter. These elk made it through the winter, as I watched them leave for the high country in June. I also took the elk bales of hay over by the Granite Falls, as the feed in the deep snow is all gone. The elk are eating the hay we put out and are doing well. Brave is pretty well crippled up. Still giving him medicine.

Some college students came in from Utah. One of them had trouble breathing. I took her in my sleigh to one of the summer cabins to rest up. She was having as asthma attack. Lucky I came along!

Kristi gave me more trouble and I worked on it...26-30 inches of new snow in two days. Peg and I enjoyed Easter Sunday dinner. Snowed all day.

April seems to be no different. More snow. On April 6, I saw the first robin of spring. Or so we hope. Heard and saw about six avalanches on Terrace Mountain. Cleaned pool and fed trapped elk. Saw bobcat and marten tracks today. Coyotes have been very active. On April 14, Peg and I went to town for the first time in weeks. Peg skied up the trail with Ruth, the camp cook, who took care of our ducks. Always easier going down than back up!

Larry and Janet brought some people up from Alaska to see the ranch. The owners are thinking of selling it. We have mixed feelings about this.

Things have been rough but we have accumulated many happy memories here.

END OF AN ERA

April 26-30: Went fishing Thursday and saw trout but could not catch any. Jim Lakey, one of our hunting clients, sent me a new handmade Green River style hunting knife [made by Dan Denahay] for a gift last week. Really nice.

Caught four trout today.

Took Peg by sleigh 10 miles to our truck, as she needs to see a dentist, been having jaw and head problems. She will stay with the Moores overnight or two nights.

I met Bob Wiley, who is a log cabin builder and who went over our plans to enlarge our old homestead.

Picked up Peg on the highway with snowmobile and sleigh. She had to have all four wisdom teeth pulled out. That was her problem!

Peggy is feeling better now after her teeth extractions. She will go to Salt Lake City to spend a week's visit with her mother.

May 10-20: Beautiful, clear and sunny day, lots of melting. I took Peg to the highway where her Mom will drive her to Salt Lake City for the week. Took them up to see the new property we bought on Camp Creek.

Water getting high on Granite Creek. Fed snowbound elk three bales of hay yesterday. Peg still in Salt Lake, will return Sunday.

May 23: Peg got back Sunday!

May 27-31: Saw a bear below the ranch. Had a bear permit and tried to get him with my .44 Mag. handgun Ruger single action but he outran me. What a sight! Ha! Saw mountain sheep.

June 1-10: Road to ranch and hot springs still snowed in. Larry came by to plow snow with his dozer. We opened the springs for the summer season. The parking lot is still deep with snow. Shane and I went bear hunting the other night. No luck! Saw moose, elk, ducks, beavers. I've been working on our new property, getting home late at night. We still don't have a hired man at the pool. The fellow who was supposed to take the job was shot in the head and killed! I didn't receive any details about how this happened. We tried to learn what we could, but for now that was all we could learn. It struck home. Just how dangerous is our work in Wyoming?

June 11-25: Yesterday on my way home, I saw my first new-born moose calf this year. During this time I went with Larry to drive 50 head of horses from the Pinedale Ranch back to the Granite Ranch. It required two days to cover that distance on horseback. Larry, Don, Scott, Shane and I had to drive them 60 miles. Last of the big western cowboy horseback drives?

I worked at our Camp Creek Ranch and saw a bighorn ram go right through our property. Weather has been rainy and cool. Awful! Met with the builder this morning at our new property. Finally, the weather turned sunny as July approaches.

In July, I began working for Granite Ranch. Larry's sons Shane and Scott killed a cinnamon-hued, bear, then Don got a big black bruin. Television film-makers, including Wolfgang Bayer, began making a movie about beavers, using the ranch as a headquarters. While Peg worked at the pool every day, I worked on the ranch, shoeing horses, and clearing brush on the new property. I'm up and in the saddle every morning at 5:30 a.m. wrangling horses that are turned out every evening to graze. I don't quit until 6.30 p.m.

While chasing horses in the early morning, I saw lots of deer and moose, and a five-point bull elk. I also took two guests out fishing, catching trout on Trail Creek. On one day we went to Mac-Leod Lake which is usually good fishing. But for some reason, we couldn't catch a fish. At over 10,000 feet elevation such waters can be temperamental but this was a first to not catch fish at MacLeod. It has been hot lately. Maybe the glacial water is too warm? But at

10,500 elevation, it really shouldn't have been too warm for these fish to lose their appetite. A mystery.

In August, Peg's mother and Deane came to visit for three days and had a good visit with them. I took a pack trip out for Larry, gone five days, scouting for game but we saw little. It seems elk and moose, in particular, hole up in north slope pines in hot weather and are difficult to find. I don't make much money on these high country horse pack excursions for Larry's hunt camp but they are great learning experiences.

In early September, I went to set up Larry's hunting camp. We took 25 pack horse loads in during a three-day period. I took a sheep hunter for a scouting trip. The hunter gave me a hand-made knife that he makes, a famous bowie knife! Brave has been getting weaker and weaker and can't walk...I don't know what keeps him alive. We have been carrying him around where he needs to go for the past two months. He is now 14 years old and I raised him from a pup. Snow-white German shepherd, 120 lbs. and he has been my pal for all his years.

Brave, my pal, died at 10 a.m. on Sept. 8. He was in no pain. He waited for me to get back from hunting camp before he died. He was a proud dog, strong and white as snow with a black nose, weighing 100 lbs. or more when in prime condition. He was born near the Canadian border and I bought him when he was six weeks old. He spent the first part of his life with me at my parents' home in Pennsylvania. We had him and our basset hound, Stoney, flown to Utah when we moved from Pa. Brave was ever faithful to Peg and me to his dying day. May he rest in peace and receive his reward by the Almighty who created him. We buried Brave on Granite Creek beside our pet squirrel, Butch, in a pine grove facing the high mountains.

Sept. 10: First day of elk hunting season. Weather has been too warm for good hunting. Animals stay in shade, much of it in the north slope thickets.

Through remainder of the hunting season, the weather cooled and we found excellent hunting if we worked at it very hard. Our hunters missed a very large mule deer, a trophy, but it got away to challenge us another day. We got into the elk pretty good, as I honed up my hunting skills from the year before, working always to become a better guide and helping the clients become better and more skillful hunters. Most don't know much about horses but we can take care of the packing and wrangling, if they will listen to us and do what we tell them while on horseback. One thing we have to drill into them is to keep the rifle chamber empty (not just on safety) but know how to get the firearm out of the scabbard quickly and safely, get a shell in and be ready to shoot.

Sometimes a game animal, especially the bigger and smarter ones, only give a few seconds before they're gone! My sheep hunter saw a large ram too far away to shoot. I climbed high ledges (with some spooky drop offs as is often the case in sheep hunting) but to no avail. The big ram got away. And I wondered what I was doing up there anyway risking my life!

On Sept. 29, I celebrate my birthday. Now 40 years old!

One of our hunters shot a giant bull moose in October and we had moose steaks for dinner. My hunter also killed a huge mule deer, with an outside antler spread of 31 1/2 inches, weight about 300 lbs. One of my hunters shot a buck which fell over a cliff and we had to use a long rope to lower him out. We got back late that night.

Two hunters who were lost found their way out on Oct. 13. Sheriff's office and a helicopter had been alerted. Having a lost hunter is something every guide has to worry about in the cold, high country of the West. A guide should never leave his hunters on their own.

On Oct. 19, Erwin Bauer, veteran hunting writer for the national magazine *Outdoor Life* and his wife, came to camp to take pictures of two trophy bucks my hunters had bagged. I look forward to seeing his article. It will help hunters to realize the great game country we have here in Jackson Hole. During this time, we hired an Indian packer and wrangler. We also hired a new man to help Peg at the pool.

My hunters took five big bucks and an elk in a 12-day period when no other guides or hunters got a thing! One of my hunters also missed a huge buck. Some of these deer could likely make the Boone and Crockett North American Big Game Records but you have to hit them first.

When the last of the hunters was gone, I thought I might have sufficient time for myself to do some elk hunting. After all, I had given Larry much dedicated service for more than two years. But Larry pulled out all the horses and put them on the winter range. I could not hunt without them. Very disappointed!

On Nov. 11, Peg and I finished moving most of our belongings to our new home on Camp Creek. We had bad snowstorms, poor visibility. Made our last load this day in worst part of storms, high winds. Spent night in our new home. Right next door to the east is a state-owned elk winter feeding ground, so we can see elk, bighorn sheep, moose and deer every winter day from all our windows.

Peg and I took a hunting trip to the Meeteetse area some 130 miles to the east and spent much time making stalks in vain. The antelope simply outsmarted me on their terms. On my last day, I succeeded in bagging a nice buck after walking many miles. Peg helped me pack in the antelope. I have often wondered if she enjoys the hunt as much as I do...realistically, probably not. But she is certainly a great woman for a hunter like myself to be married to!

During Thanksgiving week, Peg and I went to her mother's place in Salt Lake City. We bought furniture there for our new home and hauled it back to our home in our horse trailer. Our new place is easier to get into than Granite Ranch. We used a four-wheel drive to break the trail in. When we did, we found that many more elk had moved into the feeding grounds next door.

We were still managing the Hot Springs, so I took in supplies to Bill [helper at the Springs] but boy, did I have a rough time try-ing to get in with snowmobile and sleigh. I had to get out the Kristi snow cat to go the final five miles. Fortunately, as December came upon us, Kristi was working for the moment. Bill is now using dogs to help police the Springs.

In the meantime, Peg and I had plenty to do at our new home on Camp Creek. As usual, we had to get ready for a tough winter, this time in a new setting, not yet tried and tested.

I called my parents (first telephone we'd had in years but still no indoor plumbing or TV) on Christmas Day. All well! We enjoyed our first Christmas in our log home, comfortable with no water leaking down the walls...at least not yet. We haven't got all the electricity hooked up but it is planned for a week hence. I've been busy trimming the willows and chokecherry brush which surrounds the house. We cut our home quite literally out of a densely vegetated hill!

After Christmas, I helped Ben feeding Camp Creek refuge elk. We fed 160 bales of hay a day using teams of horses and sleigh. Interesting thing about the wapiti [Shoshone name for these cream-colored animals]. They will feed normally if you remain on the sleigh and don't get "personal." But if you climbed off the sleigh and were to be in human form on the ground, I'm told they would stampede off the premises.

Jan. 1, 1975: Happy New Year! Weather cold and cloudy. Few

days later, had to pick up our hired helper, Bill, at the springs for his dental appointment. Saw 20-25 head of mountain sheep outside our gate. Bill stayed with us overnight and took him back to the Springs next day. From time to time we had to get supplies to him.

On Jan. 8, I answered an ad in the newspaper for a man who wanted to sell his outfitter license and business. I had been thinking about going on my own some day, especially after working so hard for Larry. I talked to Red Buscher. Sounded good to me but I'll have to study it out some more. It didn't take me long. I drove to his home in Wilson the next day to seal the deal!

The snow was piling up and I doubted I could much longer drive into our new property. It looks like snowmobile and sleigh all over again.

Peg got selected to sit on jury duty in Jackson. Don't know what that entails yet. Can't drive the truck onto property right now. On Jan. 14 Peg served jury duty and remained in town two nights. Had Monty Evans plow our road. Shoveled snow all day. Peg got home finally and most unusual, weather was so warm that snow began melting! A true January thaw.

Jan. 27-31: Peg back on jury duty. Worked on snowmobile. A big bull elk on feed ground, with 1,200 total animals. Peg back and forth on jury duty. She had to snowshoe or ski out to the road. Well-known mountain man Neil Rafferty told me of an elk calf struggling in Granite Creek. We dragged all 350 lbs. of it in a sleigh but the creature died before we could get it to the cabin to warm it up and feed it. At least we tried. In the icy, below zero cold of Granite Creek we found our jeans frozen to our waists. And I still had 18 miles to go with my body in frozen jeans to get home to Peg.

Feb. 22-28: Peg and I took a group of movie producers, including Gordon Eastman, into the Granite Canyon and Springs. On the way out, Kristi developed gear trouble and would work only in low gear. We made it but slow and late, 10 p.m. Worked on the Kristi. Most disgusting damn machine I ever bought or worked on, nothing but trouble ever since I bought it.

Purchased a nice palomino mare, likely bred I'm told, by a thoroughbred stallion. Paid $250.00 for her.

In early March, we had a serious outbreak of flu in the Jackson area.

March 20-30: I took my state outfitters' test and passed! But I learned of a problem when Dave Thomas, the local game warden, met with me and told me there was no opening for me to guide in the Hoback Canyon area. He said the other outfitters were worried about me! I had not been told that before. Well, we shall see! Some outfitters have two camps and do not use the surrounding area. They just want to control everything! I will go along with them for only so long. There are thousands of acres which could sustain much more hunting pressure.

March 29: Larry Moore died tonight about 10 p.m. from a sudden heart attack. He had been very sick from the flu shortly before. He was the first man I worked for in Wyoming. I finished working for him last fall. Larry was only 43 years old, and a good father and husband. They'll miss him. And so will Peggy and me.

I also took sick from the flu yesterday. It's the first time I've been sick since moving to Wyoming. I laid in the old cabin we bought. At least warmer than the old bunk house.

First day of April I felt a little better. I had no appetite and a fever for four days. On April 2, Peg and I attended the funeral services for Larry. He will be cremated and his ashes taken to Granite Ranch, his ranch and canyon. That's where he would like to be.

Parker and Karen Moore, ranchers from Douglas, Wyo., spent the night with us. They met at Granite Ranch and were later married.

Peg went to visit her mother in Salt Lake for three weeks, then with her mother to visit Peggy's grandmother in Lawrence, Kansas.

April 10: Snow going fast. Peg's been gone a week now! Pretty lonely here. I've been really sick with the flu the past two weeks and my back is giving me lots of pain, driving me crazy. My appetite is bad; I hardly get hungry at all. I have not been sick like this for years. All I want to do is lie down and sleep. No energy. Legs feel sore and stiff.

I've also been to town to see Janet Moore and kids, and Janet's lawyer, Phil Margules, about buying Larry's hunting camp. They want a big price, $60,000. Phil says they'll take $50,000. Lots on my mind besides being sick.

I didn't know it then but a whole new era was about to open up in my life as I sought to purchase my own prime area big game hunting camp. It would change my life. But for now, sadly, I could not come to terms with the Moores.

●●●

Teton Views, Jackson Hole newspaper:
"More on life in Granite Creek"
[Story written about Gap and Peggy following the reporters'
visit mentioned earlier.]

"Gap speculates that the Gros Ventre and Sheepeater Indians were probably the first bathers to use the Granite Hot Springs...Dr. Don MacLeod who also ran the Granite Hot Springs concession, wrote a history of the pool. He called the springs, 'a place...used by early settlers to bathe and relieve pains and aches. ' Access was by a poorly developed road up the east side [10 miles] of Granite Creek. The facility has always been owned by the Forest Service...but Dr. MacLeod and son-in-law Larry Moore operated the Springs just before Gap Pucci bought the lease in the early 1970s.

"Gap says, 'We were the first white people to ever winter

there. Forty years ago that was rugged country. Almost no one came there [hot spring] when we first started. ...I drug a piece of metal behind a snow machine to bust a trail so people could get in.' Gap and Peggy charged $1 for visitors to swim in the Hot Springs. Their first winter they made $600.

"The Springs remained undeveloped until 1933 when the Civilian Conservation Corp built a road, concrete pool, and dressing rooms. The Forest Service operated the pool for a time, sending someone out to clean the pool [algae buildup] once a week or so. [Note: Teton Views explains that the dressing rooms were never warmed by a heater. Some visitors in the dressing rooms simply sat and watched others swim because it was so cold getting into a swim suit before entering the warm water. And it was even colder getting out to dress.]

"Gap on first living quarters: 'The log bunk house at Granite Ranch was cold...snow would blow in between the logs. And we had an outhouse we had to shovel a trail to. By mid-winter it was more like a tunnel. Every Monday I'd [Gap] haul water out of Granite Creek for the week. I'd fill five-gallon milk cans and haul them in a sleigh back to the kitchen. An old wood stove heated the cabin.

'Peggy and I were alone at the ranch for days without seeing anyone else. When you blew your breath in the morning in the bunk house, steam would blow out. We'd look at each other to see whose turn it was to get up and build the fire that morning. We learned to build a fire quickly.'

"Peggy: 'We thought we'd go to town maybe once every couple of weeks but it was such a big job, such an ordeal, that we only went every six weeks. If you left a house plant or anything else that was perishable, it would be frozen by the time you got back.'

"Peggy brought a tiny Eastern gray squirrel with her from Pennsylvania and fed it with an eyedropper. Peggy named him Butchy and carried him everywhere. He would hide in her hair. Peggy said sometimes he would try to bury an acorn in my hair. Gap would feed him corn flakes. 'Butch would sit at the table with us eating corn flakes. Gap would have his bowl of cornflakes and Butchy would have his pile.'

"One time a bear knocked down the door to the Hot Springs cabin and made a mess of things. He carried off a sack of flour. Gap tracked him up the mountain by following the trail of flour.

"One night Gap forgot to close the gate to the Camp Creek Ranch located next to the state elk refuge. The next morning 400 head of elk were in here. They had the horses pinned up in a corner. They scared those horses to death!

"Despite their problems with Granite Hot Springs, Peggy has this to say about it: 'I had poignant memories of the place. For us, Granite Hot Springs was a beautiful, peaceful place. In the fall, if you climbed the rocks above it, the pool looks like a turquoise jewel surrounded by autumn leaves. Now it's known world wide. Many families come back year after year. It was a pleasant time in our lives. I hope they always preserve that place.'

"Gap: 'We had two little girls who learned to swim at the Hot Springs. We watched a whole generation of kids who came there grow up. It's nice to have those memories.'"

MY OWN HUNT CAMP

In April of 1975 I talked to Janet Moore about buying the rights to the Granite Hunting Camp and I also had a good talk with Dr. MacLeod, who is Janet's father.

April 14: There are seven mountain sheep right outside our window on the southwest slope where they like to winter and graze. They are shedding and look white now, all lambs and ewes except for one small ram.

April 18: Easter Sunday, the day our Lord was risen. Peg was still visiting her grandmother in Kansas. I talked to her on the phone. I'm still not feeling good, back bothering me bad, weak and sick, can't seem to get well. Went to Salt Lake on the 29th to pick up Peg. Back in Wyoming, we were able to drive right up to our house, the first time in a long while.

May 4: Today I met with Janet and Doc and Mrs. MacLeod to

talk about buying their hunting camp. Peg and I spent two winters and a summer working at Granite Ranch [eight months to a winter] up there. Now, we just hope things work out to return on a more permanent basis.

In May I trained our new horse Sunny. He's doing fine. I've not heard from Janet about the hunting camp.

Jim Lakey sent me the new saddle (a gift) he had made for me. It's beautiful and well made. I called him in Arizona to thank him. I worked on a new horse corral. Hummingbirds have been at our feeders. We finally got the Hot Springs pool painted.

In middle June, Mrs. MacLeod was in the hospital, very sick with cancer. We went to see her and pray for her.

July 26: We finally bought our own hunting camps! Today, I signed the papers. We bought Stilson's camps in the Gros Ventre Mountains. There are three camps, a base camp, and two high camps. The hunting area is three times the size of Granite Creek area. Old and historic camps started by Jim Simpson, then John Wort and Steve Callahan, in 1905. They were some of Jackson Hole's first outfitters. [Note: "outfitter" is the name given to the person who runs the camp and hires the guides.]

About this time I wrote a list of grievances to the Forest Service and sheriff's office about our problems in the Granite Hot Springs Canyon. I will highlight them here.

How can we patrol it? The only telephone we can count on is

20 miles away. We are the only people living in this wilderness area to enforce the law, with a hired man sometimes. We put up road sign regulations but they mean nothing to hippies and some of our local people. We are harassed about wearing firearms. The badge they gave me doesn't mean anything! Packing a pistol was necessary for Peg and I to get something accomplished and to defend ourselves in some cases. We have been threatened with bodily harm again and again, some of them drunk or on drugs. Some destruction of our own property has occurred. We keep replacing signs and barriers. What do they expect us to do? I can call and report we have trouble, or are expecting it, but we get little or no help! One night about 80 hippies descended on the Springs and what could we do? We tried calling the sheriff after driving 20 miles and no one showed. I went in person to talk with the sheriff and he told me he was short-handed. He could not promise me any protection! I told Forest Service also; after all, it's on their land. They are the ultimate managers!

My wife and I were very much alone. Would you have carried side arms? Sheriff's deputies did come one night and we ran 12 hippies out who were swimming in the nude. It was the only time sheriff's deputies came to help us. I stopped a rape one night and that only by gun point! In time, my wife and I felt we had made Granite Springs 95 per cent safer for the good people and families to use and this with little outside help.

We have been thanked by many local people and hunters this

fall for making Granite a safer place to be but I have been warned by the sheriff about using side arms to protect my wife and me. Yet, no official power is willing to do anything about it, night after night. We want some official power to issue fines and make arrests for a safer forest so that the public can use it safely. Can't we just put up a sign on a gate warning trespassers what legal action will be taken against them? I am interested in Forest Service regulations and enforcement by the federal government, not being told the problems of the sheriff's office. Can't we get something accomplished here to solve this problem for the good of all those people who want to use the Granite Hot Springs in safety?

The winter 1976 was most unusual. Very little snow here or anywhere in the local Rocky Mountains. The entire West is having a drought. There has not been a winter like this since 1923, according to what our insurance man, Garl Riggan, told me this week. Meantime, I hear from Pennsylvania that the East is having the worst snow and cold in a hundred years!

I spent the past hunting season in my own camp! We took many bull elk and buck deer. One bighorn sheep. And several moose.

I returned to the Black Hills to hunt and got my first wild turkey! It was a 25-lb. gobbler. Also three antelope and one white-tail buck. We spent Thanks giving near Sundance by the Black Hills. Had wild turkey for Thanksgiving.

On Nov. 18 we lost Stoney. Our basset hound had been sick

for about two weeks. We took him to the vet and tried all kinds of medications. But he wouldn't eat. We force-fed him but nothing helped. There was never a more lovable dog. He gave us his love and devotion 24 hours a day. He became my hunting pal, being an excellent pheasant and rabbit dog, a good retriever as well as companion in the field. He brought us lots of enjoyment and laughs in the field. He would have been 11 in March. He was, however, always Peggy's dog.

I'm thinking of Stoney. He was the last of the animals we brought from Pennsylvania. When I was away at hunting camp, he kept Peg company. He loved to watch the elk in the nearby feed ground. He was always curious about things. We laid him to rest on the southeast corner of our property, high on the hill where his spirit will be free to wander forever.

Mrs. Dorothy MacLeod died three months after Larry, her son-in-law, did. She was always nice to Peg and me. We lived close to her at Granite Ranch. She was the Boss. We will miss her very much.

THE GIRLS

As I , Gap, write these later notes, Catherine and Teresa are 30 and 28 years old, respectively. Although Peggy and I are certainly biased, we are proud of what they have become growing up in their hinterland home. Both girls were born in October (in the heart of hunting season): Catherine Oct. 13, 1978, and Teresa, Oct. 7, 1980.

In fact, I was deep in hunting camp in the Gros Ventre Wilderness when our first daughter was born. To notify me, Peggy had bush plane pilot Bob Wiley drop this note to me:

"Gap, You are the proud papa of a baby girl, 7#, born on Friday, 10-13-78. Mother and daughter are doing fine & everything under control. Peg said let the base camp know if possible. Congratulations! Bob Wiley."

Bob was a Jackson Hole friend, an inspiration to us, always supportive.

Obviously, I would have done anything to be there but many

clients depended on me being at camp. I was most grateful Peggy let me know when she did and managed to usher in our family with such grace and courage. Her mother came from Salt Lake City to be with her.

Some of the first things our girls were to see as we held them up to our window was the abundant wildlife that surrounded our ranch, such as bighorn sheep, elk, moose, mule deer, coyotes and other animals. Catherine and Teresa would hear the elk bugling and coyotes howling from their beds in our cozy log cabin.

After nursing the babies, the very first whole foods they learned to eat were, of course, wild game meat that I harvested for our table. It included bear, deer, elk, moose, bighorn sheep. Peggy used a little hand grinder to whet the meat fine enough for them to eat. We never used any store-bought commercial baby foods!

They had no close neighbors or television set, so they learned to become good pals playing with each other doing what they knew best. They are the only little girls I know who would play "outfitter guide," packing their Barbie dolls and gear on toy horses with rubber bands to hold everything in. They did fine. I taught them the diamond hitch that professional guides use to pack real horses in the wilds. They practiced packing their toy horses with the same knots. Their "wilderness" was in the back yard, way back in the willow patch where there was a fire ring. They had a grand time!

We think my personal horse, Sunny Jim, enjoyed the girls just as much as they enjoyed playing with him. He was a sorrel [reddish] hue that seemed made to carry young girls on his back. On sunny days, I would let them ride while Nino, our German shepherd followed and watched over them. Sunny would not let any adults ride except me. I rode him and guided hunters from his back for many years.

Both Catherine and Teresa learned to ride well by the time they were six. At that age they rode several times into Dad's hunting camp but there were a few scary moments crossing steep ridges and swift streams. After Sunny was retired [too old to ride], I took care of my favorite mount until his death on Feb. 16, 2003. He was 32! Average age of even a healthy horse is more like 20 years.

It was a sad day for the girls, even though they were grown up by now. They have many memories of Sunny, as do Peg and me. One we still talk about is when Catherine, age 5, and Teresa, 3, rode double on him via an old second hand Roy Rogers saddle I had bought for them. The girls were playing outfitter leading their make-believe hunters into the high mountains when Teresa decided she had to go the bathroom. As I glanced over, I saw water running down the little saddle all over Sunny. Catherine was also by now wet! The three of them seemed undaunted as they continued to lead the way to camp. When I noticed it and stopped the pack string, Teresa said, "Well, we couldn't stop Sunny and we had to get our hunters to camp."

We all had a good laugh over that one and I think even Sunny smiled over it. We still get together and talk about it.

The little Roy Rogers saddle sits in our living room along with other trophies [including big game trophies]. Sunny Jim, gentle horse and friend to our family, is buried on our ranch with a special marker. His spirit will be with us forever.

Peggy spent much time reading to the girls. They learned to do their own reading and to say their prayers daily. When they were old enough for school, it was 25 miles through rugged terrain in Jackson. We had no four-wheel drive (snow would be too deep in winter anyway), so we used snowshoes, snowmobile and sleigh to get them from our isolated ranch house. Of course, when going to town we bought food and hauled the girls and groceries together.

Sometimes the winter temperatures dropped to 40 below zero. In the winter of '78-79, it dropped to 63 below zero! When the snow got deep, the sleigh would sometimes tip over, sprawling girls and groceries everywhere. When Catherine was first taken to school [Teresa was still too young] Peggy would wrap the younger girl in a warm sheepskin and extra blankets. Teresa made the trip both ways...twice a day right along with older sister.

We would gather up all, brush snow off the girls and try to locate the buried groceries. We learned to laugh about it (we had to) and try again. Usually the next morning Nino, the German shepherd, would find the eggs frozen and we hauled them home. They were then too hard to break. We would thaw them out for the next day's breakfast.

As the girls grew, they would become involved in 4-H programs, winning ribbons at the Teton County Fair via leather crafting and tooling. Many came with Morgan and other breed show horses and barrel racing, with excellent horsemanship at the local rodeo. Peggy won ribbons and grand championships for her photography. I won prizes with my Morgan show horses, including the stallion Starless Knight, who became Teton County Grand Champion.

Those were memorable growing up years for the girls who live here even now as I write this in Jackson, a place they've learned to love. Beautiful young ladies, they work at local restaurants. As for whether they will remain here, Peg and I don't know. But they have expressed how much they enjoy the legacy and heritage which was theirs high in the mountains.

As I think back on some of the hardships we (all four of us) went through, I realize they were not insurmountable. Perhaps adversity merely strengthened our resolve. Those first years there was no running water nor indoor toilet facilities. Electricity and television came later. As soon as we could afford these conveniences [some would say necessities] we saw to it. But it may be that they were appreciated even more after not having them for so many years.

THE HOBACK YEARS

C Bar C Valley Ranch

©THE CRYSTAL IMAGE

Top: Gap packs out a client's ram after a successful hunt. Bottom: A bull elk responded to Gap's plaintive bugling, aided by a length of tubing he found on the highway.

Opposite page: Gap demonstrates the way early mountain men, including Jim Bridger, tied game meat on a horse to pack it out. Few modern outfitters know how to employ this useful technique, relying instead on canvas panniers.

132

Top: Gap leads a long packstring across the Gros Ventre River. Bottom: Gap poses with a client's kill, a full curl ram.

Opposite page, top: Peg bundles newborn Catherine up for a trip out of their Hoback cabin to the highway into Jackson. Bottom: Because October is the height of fall hunting season, Gap missed the birth of both of his daughters. Friend and pilot Bob Wiley dropped a coffee can containing this note into Gap's hunting camp to inform him of the first-born Catherine's arrival.

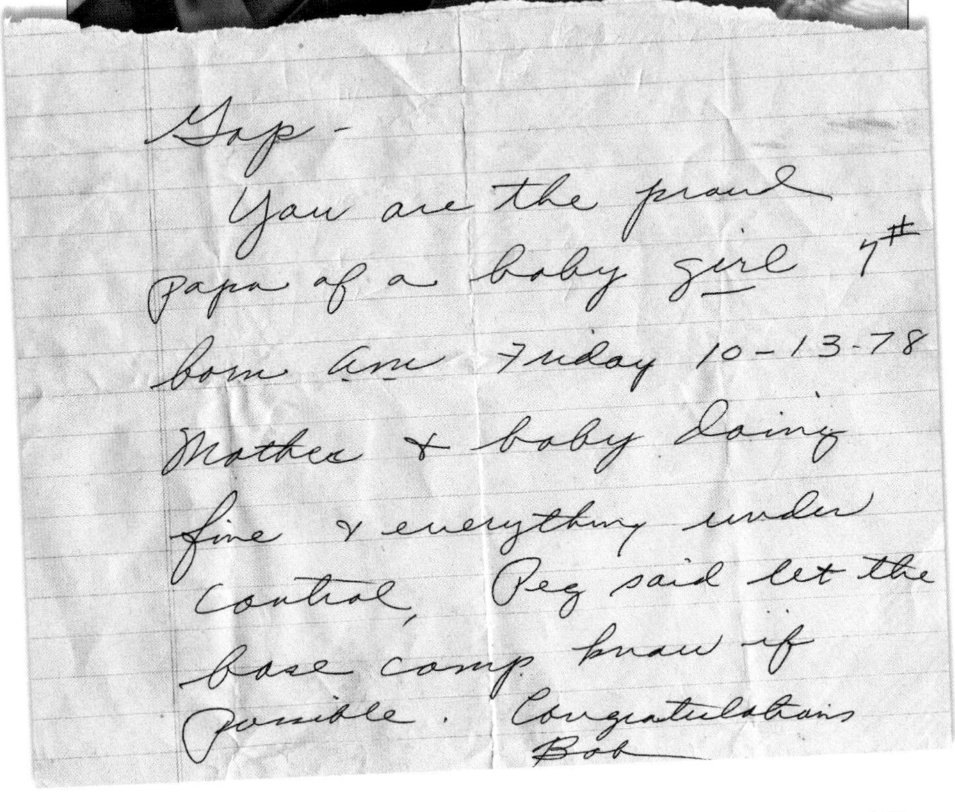

Gop —

You are the proud
papa of a baby girl 7#
born am Friday 10-13-78
Mother & baby doing
fine & everything under
control, Peg said let the
base camp know if
possible. Congratulations
Bob

Top: Peg carries daughters Catherine and Teresa on an early 1980s excursion up the Gros Ventre, accompanied by faithful companion Nino. Bottom: Gap keeps a firm hold on toddler Teresa on the back of Sunny Jim, a spirited horse that was always gentle with the girls.

Opposite page, top: Baby Teresa finds a comfortable perch on a black bear pelt, a record bear shot by one of Gap's clients. Bottom: Catherine and Teresa, with loyal dog Nino, pose with Gap. The bear pelt in the background was from a bruin Gap shot in Granite Creek.

This page, top: Gap and Peg's homestead cabin above Camp Creek. The outhouse and outside shower are seen to the immediate right of the cabin. Bottom: Teresa, left, and Catherine bathe in a tub at the Gros Ventre base camp. Note the stove to warm the water in the background.

Opposite page: Gap and Peggy's Hoback Canyon home above Camp Creek. Deep winter snow often times made getting to the highway challenging.

Opposite page, top and bottom: Leaving the gate open at Gap and Peg's Hoback Canyon home was an open invitation for wintering elk to browse the backyard.

This page, top: Gap and Catherine feed a starving elk calf that hung around the cabin during a particularly deep snow year. Bottom: Elk weren't the only animals that made the Pucci's property their winter home base. One season, 10 moose were frequent visitors.

141

This page, top: "Old Cracked Horn" bedded down. The Pucci family watched him grow from a lamb to a magnificent ram, easily identified by a crack in his horn. Bottom: A hungry ewe bumps her head against the cabin's kitchen window to let Gap know she is waiting to be fed.

Opposite page: Gap feeds multiple bighorn rams and ewes surrounding the Pucci's Hoback ranch, driven to lower elevations by winter hunger.

144

Opposite page, top: Teresa sits astride Sunny Jim, while Catherine holds the reins. Gap calls this picture "Our Family." Bottom: Gap shows his tender side as he nuzzles Michael, an orphaned colt.

This page, top: Teresa and Catherine are all smiles on the back of Sunny Jim, a great mountain horse considered a member of the family. Bottom: Teresa pats Dudley on the nose. Looking at this photo, you'd never guess Dudley liked to pull up fence posts and "damn near killed" the author when he had to shoe him.

Opposite page: Teton County Fair Grand Champion Morgan Stallion Starless Knight, draped with the American Flag and bowing before Our Saviour at a Nativity Scene at the Pucci's home.

This page, top: Catherine, age 14, holds Erin Belle, a Morgan horse named Grand Champion "Best of Show" at Teton County Fair. Bottom: Teresa displays ribbons earned at the fair for her skilled leathercraft.

147

CRYSTAL CREEK MORGANS'
Home of the *"Iron Horses"!*

"CRESCENT SILVER MIST" & CATHERINE

Catherine rides Crescent Silver Mist in a Teton County Rodeo barrel racing competition. The Morgan horse garnered "Best All Around" honors.

148

THE OUTFITTING YEARS

The National Register
of Historic Places
Wyoming Place No. 287

Wort/Gap Puchi
Hunting Cabin

BIG
WYOMING

WYOMING IS
WHAT AMERICA WAS

©THE CRYSTAL IMAGE
Jackson Hole, Wyoming

150

Opposite page, top: Gap and good friend Erwin Bauer rest near Bauer's elk shot in Crystal Creek drainage in the 1970s. Bottom: Erwin with his bull elk bagged in a 1976 hunt with Gap. Erwin was a well-known photographer who helped Gap gain international fame as an outfitter.

This page, top: Writers/photographers Erwin and Peggy Bauer, bundled up at the Gros Ventre base camp cabin. The Bauers and Puccis became lifelong friends. Both Bauers are now deceased. Bottom: Like the Bauers, outfitting cemented long-lasting friendships with Father Carl Beavers, left and Father Jaime, pictured here on a pack trip with Gap.

151

CRYSTAL CREEK OUTFITTERS VIDEO

BIG GAME HUNTING & WILDLIFE VIDEO SERIES

MAGNIFICENT WILDLIFE! Elk, Moose, Bighorn Sheep, Mule Deer, Bear! AUTHENTIC HUNTS & WILDLIFE DOCUMENTARIES! Hunter Preparation, Professional Techniques, Trophy Handling & Horsepacking — from Jackson Hole, Wyoming! — "Last & Best of the Old West."

Conservationist Mardy Murie, pictured here by her cabin in Moose, encouraged and supported Gap and Peg's fledgling outfitting business. When the Puccis released their wildlife video series and sent Mardy a copy, she responded with the note on the opposite page. Louise "Weezie" MacLeod is Mardy's half-sister.

CRYSTAL CREEK OUTFITTERS VIDEO

Gap & Peg Puchi, Exec. Producers
Star Route, Box 44A
Jackson Hole, Wyoming 83001
Phone (307) 733-6318

152

San Juan Is. Wa.
April 4

Dear Gap + Reg —
    Weezie tells me that
we are the co-owners
of a film which sounds
most interesting.
I shall certainly look
forward to some
real entertainment
when I come home in
early May!
    And it all takes me
back — remembering
the letters from
Gap — wondering about
coming west!
        I hope you are
happy about it all!
And I'll be hoping to
see you —
    Thanks + all best —
        Mardy

This page, top: Gap secures a client's elk on Dudley to pack it out of Crystal Creek Canyon. Below: Gap, on Sunny Jim, allows Dudley to graze a bit after a creek crossing.

Opposite page: From a very young age, the girls became accustomed to seeing and helping with processing the meat from a successful hunt. In the top photo, Catherine and Teresa tussle with a small antler rack while Gap stands by the family's supply of winter meat. In the bottom picture, the now older girls help drag in a carcass for the winter season.

This page, top: Teresa holds up the head of a record black bear shot by Gap's client, Tom Jones, in Granite Creek in 2006. Bottom: While the Puccis fed moose, elk and bighorn sheep that wintered near their Hoback Canyon home, not all animals were welcomed. Catherine, Gap and Teresa display a coyote that met its demise after killing the family's ducks.

Opposite page: Gap hired staff to assist in the Puccis outfitting business. Joe Garfunkle, shown in the top photo, was one of the more colorful wrangler and packers. Buster Wilson, strumming a guitar in the bottom photo, was a beloved horse wrangler who attained success in Nashville as a Country-Western singer. Sadly, he died of a heart attack in his 40s.

Opposite page, top: Pat Johnson leads an impressively long packstring into camp. Bottom: A typical hunting camp. The larger kitchen tent, shown to the right, is surrounded by a row of hunter tents, with a group gathering area around a firepit in the middle.

This page, top: What's for dinner? This may be what Benny, the Pucci's well-loved mule, is pondering as he visits Teresa in the kitchen tent. Bottom: A grizzly easily demolished an expensive, custom tent at the Crystal Creek camp, a reminder that outfitters operated in the bruins' home range.

This page, top: Gap Glasses for bighorn sheep at Crystal Creek. Bottom: An age-ing Gap is bundled against the cold as he rides Eagle, a proud Morgan horse that succumbed to old age in 2002. He lived 27 years.

Opposite page, top: Forever friends Gap and Sunny Jim stand on a ridge in front of Darwin Peak in the Gros Ventre Wilder-ness. Gap says it "just about killed" him when Sunny died, at the extremely old age of 32, in 2003. Bottom: Dudley bears a huge elk rack as Gap leads him out of the high country.

Top: Gap hunting sheep in the Gros Ventre Wilderness. Darwin Peak is in the background. Bottom: Gap shakes hands with Bart, his hybrid wolf dog.

The Old Hunter

His hair's thin and gray, his eyes now weak,
It seems much colder and more shelter he'll seek.

Mountains seem taller, valleys so deep,
and even on flat ground, it now seems steep.

His legs grow weary, his aim untrue,
He falls more often and sometimes is blue.

Campfires grow dimmer as he loses old friends,
but all the memories, he still holds within.

He's chased many rainbows, for trophies he's sought,
And now, he's older and gives it much thought.

His friends that are living, and those that are not,
Who listen to stories he tells quite a lot.

Who will remember, and who will not,
About a friend and a hunter we will miss a lot?

—Author Unknown

This page, top: The John Wort/Gap Pucci Hunting Cabin in the Gros Ventre Wilderness was placed on the National Register of Historic Places due to the tireless work of the Pucci family. The cabin was built at the confluence of Crystal Creek and the Gros Ventre River in 1929 and used by John Wort and his partner Steve Callahan as an outfitting base camp. In the 1970s, the cabin became part of the Pucci's operation when they bought Keith Stilson's outfitting business. It is the only known surviving, historic building connected to outfitting in Jackson Hole. The cabin was moved to its present location in the early 1940s. Bottom: Gap shoeing a horse.

This page, top: Illustrator Bernadette Pitera and her husband, writer Sal Pitera. The Piteras are long-time friends of Gap and Peg. Bottom: Jackson Veterinarian Timothy Gwilliam died prematurely in a work accident in 2008. He left behind loving wife Catherine, seven daughters, and many who miss his compassion and gentleness—including Gap and family.

HORSES, GOOD, BAD (AND UGLY)

One of the reasons I came west was because of my love for horses. I had learned much about them working with a great trainer, Carol Clark, in Pennsylvania, learning to shoe them and working for veterinarians. Even some outfitters and veteran ranchers don't learn to do that. But my love for horses and half a century spent with them also resulted in some mishaps. It happens with most horse/people relationships sooner or later. While I successfully broke many for riding, in the end they nearly broke me.

For example, I have a metal plate in the back of my neck and a metal full hip replacement due to my work with horses. At first, my pains led doctors to think I had Lou Gehrig's Disease. But then it was determined that while I was trying to break a horse, he broke me. Injuries affected the entire right side of my body. One fall too many!

Of course, I had many positive experiences with both mounts

and pack horses. One cayuse fell over backward into a river while we were trying to extract a Rocky Mountain bighorn sheep in a deep crevice. The horse was wedged in between rocks so he couldn't move. I had to scale down a cliff to reach him, and cut the pack saddle from him so he could turn his head up to keep him from drowning. We got the animal out alive, although it almost drowned me in the process. We found later that the pannier bags were full of water. It required a long time by the fire to dry everything out, including the saddle itself. But in time, we roped up the trophy ram for our hunter who was now one of the happiest men I ever saw.

A horse named Dudley liked to break down fences and pull down hitching racks nailed to posts. I never found a horse I couldn't break but trying to shoe Dudley, he damned near killed me. He was a 1700 lb. Belgium cross, King of the Mountain. I'd shoe him either standing or flat on his back but he could strike you with his front feet and nearly take your head off while trying to shoe him. I thought I was tough but had to admit when shoeing this horse, he was the king. He once ran right through a log fence. When shod, however, you could pack a pickup truck on him anywhere in the high country. I couldn't ride him; he wasn't meant to ride. Nevertheless, he was the toughest and most sure-footed mountain horse I ever saw. At the same time...why that horse didn't kill me I'll never know.

When tied up, Dudley either broke the halter ropes or else pulled the tree down. This was one horse willing to do most of the work assigned to him but with his penchant for a hot temper, and the fact he was reaching old age (30), I had to dispatch him. We just couldn't take any chances with anyone being hurt. When he went down, I pulled him up with a tractor but he couldn't stand. With tears in my eyes I thanked him and then took out my rifle and put him out of his misery. The King was dead!

There was the time when Ginger, 25 years old, my top pack horse, was loaded with elk quarters and decided to pull down the hitch rack which hit me square on the back of the head, knocking me down. I had a bump on my head as large as an egg plant. Lucky it didn't do me in.

Sometimes trouble with horses can be entirely unavoidable. My staff and I had just congratulated ourselves one day on getting some of our supplies and tents in to camp after a hard ride, graining, watering, hobbling and belling the horses and turning them to graze when a great clamor arose. Strangers with a pack of mules rode into camp. The first thing our big Percheron, Samson, did was kick a pannier on one of the mules. Then the fight was on. One set of horses will often take umbrage at the sudden intrusion of "foreign" stock and that was exactly what was happening.

With our loose herd of tough Morgan horses joining force and kicking, biting, and running off the strange and unwanted pack string, it sent their petrified riders down the trail toward the road. We could hear all of the yelling of those riders hanging on for dear life! What a sight that was! Soon we could no longer hear the bells of our own horses and I knew what was happening: our brood was chasing their brood the 17 miles back to base camp. Lucky for us we had tied two veteran Morgans for wrangling as we usually do and I sent one guide out to bring our horses back.

By now it was pitch black and both Bryan and his mount, Falcon, had already just ridden 17 miles to camp. I knew both could make the ride, however, and made Bryan a couple of hurried sandwiches and wished him God Speed. I made it clearly understood in such a circumstance that he could not return until he had gathered all 23 of the horses. The longer they were gone, the farther they might wander and get into trouble. I had trained him to do just that if any horses strayed and he knew it was his job, as difficult as it might be. It is always hard to drive horses, especially that many, away from the comforts of base camp but it had to be done.

Meantime, Dave and I spread our bedrolls beneath a spruce tree and hoped it wouldn't rain.

For two days we did not see Bryan. I decided to send Dave back to help him. He saddled a horse, Cimmaron that I had raised from a colt. "Don't come back until you find Bryan and the horses!" I admonished him. He knew I could depend on him to do just that. When he left, I had no horses left but continued to set up camp for the coming hunting season. One more day went by. Finally the next morning, I could hear the bells approaching. Boy, was I relieved to see them! We got the string in the corral, ate a supper of elk steaks and were happy to be in bed that night and hear the coyotes singing as the boys told of their three-day adventure to get our horses back.

I told the boys I was proud of doing what they had to do. They had reason to be proud of themselves. What they did was good old-fashioned horse wrangling, the kind you don't see every day. In fact, you rarely see it anymore. It made for a display of determination and classic savvy with horses that the three of us will always remember for a job well done.

One of my friends, Larry Moore, also had some tough experiences with pack horses. One day he got thrown and lay in a heap. When he got up, he complained of a sore shoulder. I said, "Sore shoulder? I thought you were dead!"

Many have said that guides and packers have something wrong with their heads. It is true that a good day of packing horses means at least one wreck of some sort before you get to camp. Sometimes it was not entirely the fault of the horses, like the time we had an avalanche block the trail and we had to figure out some way to get around it. Something seemed to always make getting to camp more than mere routine. Most often, however, it was the horses themselves.

We had one wrangler named Jerome "Buster" Wilson working for us, a great guide and horseman, whom we loved for his trick riding and colorful personality. He would mount from the rear of the horse and do other stunts designed to keep us entertained. He was a tall, handsome and daring lad with a comical western flair. I asked his mother why the nickname Buster and she said, "Because he busts everything he touches." But he brought much comic relief to camp when the weather was bad or we were resting in camp. He did bust things he touched around camp but we forgave him each time he played his guitar. Buster was from a good Mormon family in California. He was raised on a church ranch that his father ran. With his love for singing and guitar, he went off to Nashville and was on television's Hee Haw. He later married a former Miss America. He died much too young at age 45 from a heart attack. He was like a member of our family. I miss him!

Some wrangling challenges seem simple enough. Hobble the horses at night and put bells on them. But horses like to wander when they are hungry—apparently seeking different feed from thistles to browse—and can be difficult to find in the morning. If they hang around camp, the bells can keep one awake. But we cannot get along without horses in this wilderness and we learn to take good care of them. Like having barley and alfalfa cubes on hand when they finish a rough day. Such feed cannot just be tossed on the ground or the horse will take dirt into his system. Many hunters and most of the general public do not realize the special care which must be taken in dealing with pack and saddle mounts.

As an outfitter, I try to hire good wranglers. We had one kid appear a day late for the job and some wanted to teach him a lesson by letting him go. But when I saw he knew how to shoe horses and display quality horsemanship, a great guide and packer, I had to keep him. (This incidentally, was Buster Wilson.) We worked on him being on time and he panned out very well. People who can work with horses are a must in any hunting camp.

Such a hand is also very valuable to ranchers and outfitters when drives are made. One went 60 miles from Pinedale to Hoback country. As mentioned, I was on one of those drives. It's like the movie *Lonesome Dove* and the cowboy movies, only more so since we are talking about the real thing here, not make believe. On one drive we had no water and little food. It was all right. You've got to be rugged enough to do what you've gotta do.

You also have to get over some habits, like wanting to drink every time you're thirsty on a dusty trail. You learn it won't kill you to do what you've gotta do.

Sometimes a horse disappears for a time. Such a cayuse was Goliath, our big Morgan and Percheron cross breed draft animal. The horse collapsed on the 17-mile ride from base camp on Gros Ventre Canyon to our hunting camp high in the wilderness. Goliath remained on the ground for eight days. A veterinarian couldn't get him up. A suggestion was made to give him a helicopter ride to the vet's quarters but the United States Forest Service wouldn't let us use a chopper in the wilderness area. Then the horse vanished and we never saw him again. The mystery was never resolved even though many guides, cowboys and myself searched for his bones for several years.

Dudes coming in often fear their mount. I feel horses can discern that fear. If you can gain enough confidence with your mount to feel at peace, so does your equestrian friend for the day. I've seen hunters have to dismount every few miles and some actually fall off. My first concern has to be the hunter's safety and comfort but it would appear some make it more difficult than it has to be. True, there are things to learn besides balancing in the saddle. If the horse is going up steep terrain, you want to give it enough rein to lift its head and step forward. The tendency is to pull the reins tighter, pulling the horse backward. But the rider should hang onto the mane and lean forward rather than reining backward. The same is true with climbing onto the horse. Lean your body into it and place weight on one leg. Don't just pull on the saddle horn and roll it onto you.

Good horsemanship comes with experience but much comes with attitude. You must command your mount and show it who is boss...but the same way you would with a child. Equus caballus doesn't always see things the way you do. A burned out stump ahead may appear as a black bear. A motorbike's shiny glint may appear as something not only unknown, but something to fear. That sinking feeling in a small swamp may seem to be as quicksand. The rider's job is to not take his mount anyplace dangerous, of course, but if the animal thinks it is, perception is everything. One place your mount will not realize danger is on a slippery side slope. If the horse slips, it will fall towards the hill. This could break your leg if still in the stirrup. Slippery side hills would be better negotiated up and down rather than moving parallel to the ridge top.

Obviously, the rider must learn to show good judgment where he/she takes his animal. A good mountain horse will take good care of you but sometimes it is best to dismount on steep slopes and walk your horse up or down nasty terrain. Watch your guide and do as he does. Be patient and use your best judgment.

If the horse balks, you must assess the situation: is he frightened? Use patience. Reassure him with soft talk. If rebellious, try to determine why. Has a rope or reins caught on a tree limb? Or inside haunches and legs? That's the way rodeos make a horse buck. However, a horse should be broken to tolerate ropes and gear placed between legs and body, as all the packing is done with ropes and gear around and under the body. They should be used to it. But if the animal balks, gentle reassurance never hurts a thing.

Is the horse just being ornery? If so, you may have to show it you won't put up with that. Try to bite you when bridling? Figure it out. Don't beat on a horse's head, or they get shy of things about the head and become more difficult to bridle. But if your means of transportation gives out along the trail (steep, or perhaps with a heavy rider) you must be sensitive enough to give it rest. If in doubt, do the thing that shows compassion for your mount.

I've especially come to love the Morgan breed of horses. They're strong mountain animals, sure-footed, as are most mules. But I'm a traditionalist and prefer horses for riding and as beasts of burden. I have a 31-year-old Morgan named Silver which just keeps going. Remember, a horse is old at 25, same as a man at, say, 75.

A Horse's Prayer

Feed me, water and care for me, and when the day's work is done, provide for me with shelter...talk to me. Your voice means as much as the reins. Pet me sometimes that I may serve you more gladly and learn to love you. Do not jerk the reins and do not whip me when going uphill...give me a chance to understand you...if I fail to do your bidding, see if something is wrong with harness or feet...give me free use of my head...

Do not overload me or hitch me where water will drop on me. Keep me well shod. Do not take away my best defense by cutting off my tail...

I cannot tell you when I am thirsty, so give me clean, cool water often. Give me all possible shelter from the hot sun, and put a blanket on me when I'm not working but when I am standing in the cold. Never put a frosty bit in my mouth; first warm it by holding it a moment in your hands. I try to carry you and your burdens without a murmur, and wait patiently for you long hours of the day or night. Remember that I must be ready at any moment to lose my life in your service.

And finally, O my Master, when my useful strength is gone, do not turn me out to starve or freeze, or sell me to some cruel owner...but do thou O Master, take my life in the kindest way, and your God will reward you here and after. You will not consider me irreverent if I ask this in the name of Him who was born in a stable.

Amen.

COOKS, GOOD, BAD (AND UGLY)

Of all the people you might meet in a hunting camp, the most interesting—and distracting—are undoubtedly the cooks. They come in all sizes, shapes, philosophies... and idiosyncrasies. Most know how to make "cowboy coffee" [always strong]. You cannot run a hunting camp without a good cook and they seem to know it. They are the boss of the kitchen tent and they let you in on it. You do things their way. Even if it means they haven't adapted to the wilds. For example, I asked one cook to make me a peanut butter sandwich. She put it in with a Hershey candy bar; getting tossed around in the saddle bag half the day, the bar turned to liquid. I poured it out. At least an apple was edible.

On the other hand, a cook is not in the comfort and security of his/her own home. One cook carried a pistol on her hip as she fed the troops, not so much to keep bears away, she said (although that might be a plausible reason) but for wolves. The Homo sapiens variety...

She said and I quote: "This is just in case any of you get ideas." No one was likely to. She was a burly woman minus any particular female charms, physical or otherwise. I think she must have read too many magazine stories about lecherous old men. We had old men in camp, to be true, but I don't know any who exhibited the tendencies she had in mind. Nevertheless, for the full season she worked with us she carried that pistol on her hip.

A second reason to favor a firearm was bears. Eventually to keep bears out, I had to encompass the cook tents at each camp with an electric fence. It carried 7,500 volts in seven strands of wire. But the cook still insisted on packing the pistol. Before the fence, one grizzly entered a tent even though it had no food in it and tore the tent apart. One thing bears seek out is flour but this particular tent had no flour in it. Before the wire, we had two different bears in the food tent: one was shot in the kitchen and the other in the guide tent. Bullet holes in the tents were always a conversation piece with each new group of hunters.

I explained our adventures with bears in camps, with much advice from many sources. It seems everyone was a bear expert. Much of it didn't work.

One cook weighed about 325 lbs. and she had to be launched into the saddle from the back of a pickup truck. If getting off during the trek, it required several hunters to hoist her back on. One young lass with a Miss America body wanted to tan herself (completely) on a Crystal Creek sandbar. She did so...for several seconds...until I read her the rules. No liquor in camp either.

One cook was so good she went on to serve members of one of New York's City's finest elite families. Another prepared a dozen T-bone steaks by boiling them. "That's what they told me to do in cooking school," she said. They were so incredibly tough I had to throw them all out. Add to that the cook who caught the tent on fire. It seems one cook opened the propane valve before lighting the match. The explosion blew the cook out of the tent. I actually witnessed her flying out.

Ironically, we had another incident with a tent fire. Even when awakened and aware of the fire, one hunter just lay in his cot, yelling "Fire! Fire! Fire!" With the tent roof fully aflame, this hunter never moved from his cot. When the camp staff poured water on the tent roof, the hunter did not move, even though drenching wet. He appeared to be almost drowned. But perhaps more amazingly, two professional firemen not far from the blaze slept through the whole thing!

No one was injured. But the first-time tent was, of course, a total loss. I try to buy tents which are not flammable but with a profound propane explosion, heat simply disintegrates about anything used in camping.

[Wixom note: Gap had his tents custom made by Springbar Tents in Salt Lake City. Even large ones are easy to put up at night;

they hold together better than other tents I've ever used in wind, leave plenty of space to work in and are relatively light. Inventor Jack Kirkham had conceived a new concept in tents using tension bars around the edges so that poles were not needed in the tent's middle, nor long poles that needed threading through loops. I also favor Springbar tents and have used them for all my work when guiding people outdoors.]

LOST HUNTERS AND MORE

I'm not much at memorizing poems but there is one by Robert Frost, "Stopping by the Woods on a Snowy Evening," which just won't go away. The last lines go like this:

> The woods are lovely, dark and deep.
> But I have Promises to keep.
> And miles to go before I sleep.
> And miles to go before I sleep.

I would recite this poem often while riding back to camp at dark after a busy day of guiding. No other work of art describes the challenge of a hunting outfitter better than this. My job with all my guides was to keep our clientele safe. Sometimes it isn't easy. Dudes, even experienced hunters (mostly from flatlands with little experience in the high and rugged Rocky Mountains) can become lost in a hurry. I have to constantly remind myself which arroyo or ridge I took to get where I am. It is one reason why Wyoming requires every non-resident hunter in designated wilderness areas to have a guide. One guide is required for every two hunters and the former makes certain he keeps track of the latter. And keeps them healthy and safe.

But on one occasion a veteran outdoorsman friend of mine, Dr. MacLeod, his grandsons and myself were called in with Buster Wilson to find a hunter who had reportedly broken his leg. It was after dark on a very cold October night. I fired my pistol three times [standard distress signal in the outdoors] and heard a single shot in return. Because of our vigilance and also that of the hunter, he was rescued and able to return to normal life. I had to keep my promise to all hunters that every effort will be made to bring them back to civilization in one piece. We got this hunter out of the woods only with diligent mountain skill rescue effort.

But sometimes even a guide gets lost. An employee of mine in 1985, Jim Murray, was sent packing elk out and into town to buy supplies and did not return when expected. The 17-mile trek back to base camp and 38 subsequent miles to Jackson is not without its perils. But we learned he made it safely—and was in fact, seen at a feed store. Then he vanished from the Earth. He was never seen again. No body was found. One of his horses was located dead two years later but the Teton County Sheriff's Office reported it as mysterious disappearance and closed the case file on the man. He had left his extra horse at base camp, along with his saddle, pistol, bedroll and dog. I submit that this is just not normal for anyone and especially for guides who care so much for their belongings. There was no sense of closure for his friends and fellow guides. Yet, there was nothing we could do about it.

WRANGLING—WITH THE LAW

Of all the challenges faced by a hunting outfitter, the toughest came to be complying with federal regulations. The Forest Service said I had to, in effect, take the wilderness out of everything. They micro-managed the outfitter's business and know-how. Game meat had to be hung 15 feet off the ground, and at least 200 yards from camp, ostensibly to avoid contact with bears. This was so far away from where we were sleeping that we didn't know if a bear was working to get it. We put out bait for black bears but couldn't shoot a grizzly. The joke in camp was that with this protected species... you could shoot it if in self-defense. But you have better have the bite and claw marks to prove it.

Everything had to be packed in by horse. It took 21 days of packing over the long trail to get three new wilderness camps set up and the same to take them down. Packing camps in and out takes longer than the hunting season in my area. When I started, the season was 80 days. It was a matter of rugged endurance to make a living. You couldn't have any quit in you. Of course, I loved my work. To me it was an adventure overall, not an ordeal. But as much as you loved it, you had to make a profit to continue. In later years it was almost more than you could handle even with good help and people at home doing book work, including Peggy and the girls. There was the grocery shopping, cooking, book work and planning.

There was, on the surface, little time for anything but work. One morning a blizzard blowing some 60 miles per hour knocked trees over and some tents collapsed. All of them had to be checked constantly. Some trees had horses tied to them. All 30 horses and hunters, 14 with staff, had to get out of the high camp at 9,000 feet elevation, a challenge even to great mountain horses.

One factor some hunters don't account for in the price charged by an outfitter is the weather. It can't be controlled and yet it must be factored in, not only for safety of the clientele but to keep a camp comfortable and safe.

I also took time during the winter to try and save wildlife even though it had no direct bearing on my business. I saved seven elk one time which were trapped in deep high country snow. I couldn't get the Wyoming Game and Fish Department to do anything about it. They don't do salvage operations. Yet, I felt I couldn't watch them die. Another time I tried to save a calf elk only to have it die at the cabin door. Another calf bedded in a ladies outhouse near the hot springs to get through the winter. I fed it every day until springtime and went off healthy and well. You can save them with hay. Grass and hay are an elk's natural food. Incidentally, none of these game animals were within my hunting area.

I started professionally guiding in Jackson Hole in 1973. During my 38 years I estimated riding horseback some one thousand miles, May through November. I loved most of it—except for all the government regulations. One frustration was every year not being able get the Wyoming Game and Fish Department to help in rescuing stranded or starving wildlife. One time I hauled a calf elk out of Granite Creek in the sub-zero cold of January. I had to use sleds, ropes and a come-along to get him out and spent many hours rescuing wildlife in similar life and death situations. Many times I hauled hay to starving animals. Wild sheep were often hand-fed by me right beside our Hoback cabin. A picture of it ran in *Outdoor Life* magazine.

It seemed the state didn't care about salvage operations. The state would feed elk only if they were on the feed grounds, and then not enough!

POLITICAL ENTANGLEMENTS
by Hartt Wixom

———

Gap and Peggy have been involved in many crusades to improve conditions for hunters, guides and outfitters. When the state decided to shorten the elk hunting seasons and ban baiting for bears one year, Gap questioned if rules made from "ivory towers" were not hurting the sport of hunting. Those who made a living at it understood very well. But there was more than that. He asked if shortening a hunting season, long a goal of the anti-hunting element, was really the best thing for either the game or those who hunt it. Big game animals must, of course, be harvested to keep them within the ability of the range to feed them. Hunting is one of the tools to do this.

For Gap, hunting is also an American privilege—along with owning a gun—and the right to hunt is up there with the highest of God-given principles. Peggy backs him up.

It has always been acknowledged in the realm of hunting

philosophy that it is the state (Wyoming Game and Fish Department in this instance) who manage the game. The federal government in the way of U.S. Forest Service and U.S. Bureau of Land Management might have dominion over the terrain and even maintain the habitat; but it has long been the state which sets the rules for hunting the wildlife living upon it. Even private landowners who might legally keep the hunting public out cannot regulate the game animals which might happen to wander upon their land.

So when Gap and his fellow outfitters went to Cheyenne to see if they could alter wildlife management procedures, both tradition and prevailing law were against them. The outfitters did not prevail. The state continued to manage its wildlife and to shorten seasons when they wanted in the high country. In addition, the state allowed hunting in Jackson Hole right alongside highways when snow drives the animals to lower elevations. Gap asks, why do this if the WGFD goal is to keep too many elk from being killed?

In any event, Gap and the Jackson Hole Outfitters Association had made a statement. They asked a difficult question: did the WGFD really know whether elk herds were subsiding, or were they more concerned with overt public relations? Catering to the anti-hunting element? For example, in the realm of fishermen, a biologist once told a group of anglers he would continue planting a certain species of fish (not desired by the fishermen) because it was brightly colored and "anglers could readily see it. With these fish," said the biologist, "everyone knows the fish are there and will quit complaining to the governor that we are not doing our job." Likewise, those stocking the fish said they would continue to dump them alongside the highway where they could be easily seen and caught. "Fewer complaints" was the goal.

But is this good fish and game management?

Hunters often asked if the outfitters didn't know about supply and demand far better than those sitting in a city office 400 miles away. Some asked, but were the outfitters far-sighted enough to have significant input...or were they thinking only of their pocketbook? Gap has this to say: "We would not be in the hunting business very long if we didn't know how to manage and harvest only the surplus every year. We can see firsthand if the game populations are diminishing and if they are, it would be unwise to our own interests if we continued to over-hunt them." That was the message Gap and his associates took to the Wyoming state capitol. Gap maintains that what is good for the outfitters is also good for the general public. Can the state, or anyone, find a flaw in this argument?

Gap had many other concerns about the management of big game by the Wyoming Game and Fish Department. One was confusion for non-resident hunters with drawing elk tags. It seemed that the regulations varied with numbers of elk licenses to be issued and how to put in for the draw. Gap feels that decisions were being made via lobbying and paper shuffling in the capital city rather than consulting the Wyoming/Jackson Hole Outfitters Assn. about actual grassroots conditions in their elk hunting areas. Why not make applying for a hunting tag easier rather than more difficult?

Another issue was banning bait for bears. This one might not look right to the "tree huggers" looking at it on paper. A city dweller might liken it to shooting fish in a barrel, watching with gun over bait. But Gap and every outfitter in the woods, Wyoming or elsewhere, knows how difficult it is to happen upon a bear by chance while walking around the 5,000 square miles of its wooded habitat. With bait, you simply have a chance. Bears are not that naive; the harvest figures still show a relatively low number are removed from the population each year. If baiting is so successful as practiced in the past, hunters would have killed them all years ago. Looking at bear depredations in Gap's area, bear numbers are at an all-time high. They cause many problems when becoming numerous, as many in bear country already know.

It is much like the deer and elk hunts. Gap maintains that while some clamor for no hunting, statistics show that if a certain percentage of the animals are not removed every year, they would eat themselves out of house and home. Scientific game management calls for removing the surplus annually. It is the winter feed itself, the rangeland, which must be managed. If it is gone (over-eaten) the animals which depend on it are also gone.

MEMORABLE COMPANIONS

In my outfitting days I have met some colorful characters. They have left me with many memorable moments. Some I worked with closely. There was Tom Lamb. Tom asked me to watch over his mountain cabin while he was gone. Later, I saw a light in his place and someone walk in that I didn't recognize. I opened the door and suspecting foul play, drew my pistol. I walked in closer and saw a strange man at the table. Just as I was about to demand who he was and why he was here, pistol in hand, I realized it was...Tom Lamb!

Tom was dressed for the cold with a sheepskin around his head. When I recognized him, we both began laughing. From then on, we laughed every time we saw each other.

But, he did have to agree with me. I was doing what he asked of me. I took good care of his place.

However, one of the most colorful people I ever worked with was Joe. Joe Garfunkle. When he arrived as a wrangler, he confided he was the "black sheep" of his family. He looked as if coming from a past era, an Old West trapper. In fact, when he wasn't working for me in the Fall, he was trapping in the winter along with his wife in Arizona. She later ran off with a truck driver. She took all the traps with her and skinned the coyotes to make clothing for herself. She left him with nothing but a feeling of emptiness.

When he arrived at my place, he was driving a truck that looked like it had been attacked by a grizzly bear. From front to back it was dented and smashed with no bumpers and mostly hand-made parts. One day I asked Joe for a ride to town. There was no dash board and exposed wires ran throughout the interior. Joe touched two of the wires together to start the engine. If you wanted to play the radio, it was under the seat and again, you hooked two wires together. Then he informed me that, at times, the brakes did not work. He said he had hit a cow one morning on the Gros Ventre Road. (Once, when he'd had one drink too many, I bailed him out of jail.)

Well, as we drove up the canyon road, he had to keep plugging wires together to keep going. There was no guard rails and drop offs along the way plummeted in places more than 500 feet into the Gros Ventre River. I didn't think I'd live through it but we finally got to Jackson. It was a normal 45-minute drive but this day it took us 2 ½ hours.

In town, when it appeared the brakes were not working, I began to pray. I asked Joe how we were going to stop this thing at the first light. As we approached the red light, Joe jumped into position, disconnected some of the visible wires and slowed the truck. At this point, I thought of jumping out of Joe's monster truck while we were still moving. But as we neared the guy in the truck ahead of us, Joe opened the door with one hand on the steering wheel and began dragging his feet. Finally we came to a stop in front of Max and Helen's Trapper Motel without killing anyone. So far.

As we tried to decide what to do next and hope no cops had witnessed our adventure thus far, traffic was backed up behind us to the town square elk arch. It was the height of the tourist season and this was the only road through Jackson Hole to Yellowstone Park. Everybody was yelling at us and they were not nice words. We finally made the decision to push the monster into the motel parking lot and did so to loud applause.

We could not get the truck started again. There was no key to turn and we connected and disconnected all the wires we could find. So, we left the truck at the motel and caught a ride to my ranch another 25 miles away. Joe was still convinced it was a good truck and that he could start it, but I convinced him to call my friend at the Flat Creek Garage. He towed it into his shop and later told me, "In all my years I've never seen anything like this. There are wires everywhere, and no key."

Joe was invited to the shop where he and Mike got it started once again. But then you couldn't kill the damn thing. Without a terrible struggle.

Later, Joe offered me a ride. I said, "Forget it. I'll walk."

I still hear from some of my old hunters but a number have gone to the Great Beyond to be with their Maker. I hope I have made a difference in their lives. I hope they have great memories of God's High Mountain Country in Jackson Hole, Wyoming! Perhaps our trails will cross again. I sent many hunters home with fine big game trophies but most of all, it was memories of a wonderful adventure.

There were many memories, too, for our own family. I have not previously mentioned that we kept a pet goat. All good Sicilian Italians should have a pet goat! Ha! We also had besides a squirrel, dogs and ducks, peacocks and chickens which were part of our family. These kept me busy at home but more than that, they were pets for the girls and welcome companions for all of us.

We also had a memorable companion in the Bible. Three of my favorite scriptures from Psalms are as follows:

Psalm 71: Cast me not off in my old age; as my strength fails, forsake me not! And now that I am old and gray, O God forsake me not!

Psalm 103: Man's days are like those of grass, like a flower of the field he blooms. The wind sweeps over him and he is gone.

Psalm 118: Blessed is he who comes in the name of the Lord!

Psalm 121: I lift up my eyes toward the mountains. My help is from the Lord who made Heaven and Earth.

A MATTER OF HISTORY

by Hartt Wixom

———

Gap and Peggy did much to promote the history of the Jackson Hole area, one of them preservation of historic buildings such as the John Wort Cabin (dating to 1929) for its outfitting significance. Wort outfitted near the confluence of the Gros Ventre River with Crystal Creek, near the site of Gap's hunting camps, and all who knew of it wanted to preserve the cabin. Gap says the U.S. Forest Service, beginning in 1970, tried to have the cabin removed. But Gap and Peggy's argument was that it was "not just a cabin. It was history!" The people of the area agreed with Gap and Peggy. It was preserved for its value as the beginning of the outfitting business in Jackson Hole. Note: a large hotel in downtown Jackson now carries the name Wort. Old-timers know where this nomenclature comes from. Tourists may simply wonder how it got such a strange name.

As coordinator for the National Register of Historic Places, Gap and Peggy had much to do with getting the historic site considered and approved. Peggy says in a letter dated Oct. 9, 1989, while her husband was at Hunting Camp, that she had much correspondence with the NRHP to see that they understood what the outfitting business meant to the history of Jackson Hole. Her work paid off in setting this cabin site apart in the national register, the only site in the nation at the time honored for its role in the establishment of outfitting/hunting in America, and in northwestern Wyoming. The site is now known as the John Wort/Gap Pucci Hunting Cabin." Says Gap, " I feel it is a great honor to be named with someone as vital to the area's history as John Wort."

Likewise, Gap made five hunting videos which brought a spotlight to the Jackson Hole region and its importance in hunting, aesthetically, recreationally and economically. They are "High Country Elk Hunter," "Wild Wyoming Outfitting Country," "Trophy Care," Bighorns of Wyoming" and "Bears, Bears, Bears."

One hunting fan wrote after viewing the five videos: "You tell it like it is."

In his videos, Gap gives many tips on finding and taking trophy game and how to pack it out, minus panniers (almost unheard of in the commercial outfitting business) via ropes alone—as Jim Bridger and the mountain men did it in the early 1800s. He shows how to tie a Diamond Hitch among others and how to pack for those long treks into rugged mountain country. A writer says, "Your attitude [goal] to illustrate how to follow the legendary Jim Bridger's methods...preserving this bit of history, makes your

194

operation tops. He adds, "All those that view your hunting videos will learn, enjoy, and nearly live with the actual events for years to come."

In a special tribute he added this: "You folks, Gap and Peg, with your truthfulness and convictions are to be admired."

—Erv Malnarich [owner] *

Outfitter and Guide Home Training Course

*Erv, a longtime Montana outfitter, is now deceased.

Gap's "Last Round-Up:" Spring bear hunting at age 73, after recent
neck and hip replacement surgery.

THE LAST ROUND-UP

Now, in my middle 70's I, Gap, am still breaking horses, guiding, packing and riding over long distances. After one fall too many, I have a five-inch plate in my neck, bone graft, and 10 screws holding my damaged neck together. I also had a full hip replacement on my right side. My joints often ache with pain. As I write this, the scent of mortality is beginning to set in for the first time. Once strong, alert, swift, I am reminded of the words of the poet Wordsworth: "it is believed by all that many and many a day he thither went, and never lifted up a single stone!"

My eyes began to go. Macular degeneration, according to the doctor. Surgery needed. If out hunting, I can't steady the crosshairs like I used to. "Going wild" is gone forever. I find myself looking up to the sky, the sun, the clouds and listening to the wind as I try to see elk and eagles, as I have done for the past 40 years.

I am now going to feed the bighorn sheep and my aging family of Morgans. My beloved buckskin mule just died at age 37. We have had him since he was a three-year old. I still have Ginger, my 34-year-old lead pack horse, and my 31-year-old Morgan saddle horse, Silver. I care for them all with great compassion. They all worked for me so hard and now they deserve their retirement until they go on to the Big Pasture. Without them it would have been impossible to go where we had to go in all kinds of weather in the high mountains, often at risk to their lives. A few did not make it to old age.

Just Passin' Through

Rode up to Wort's old livery barn;
Steve Callahan was there
Said, "Get down, son; chat awhile.
And give your horse some air.
Might just as well spend the nite."
I said, "Thanks; that's what I'll do.
Tomorrow I'll be heading out,
'Cause I'm just passin' through.

Well, sixty years have come and gone,
And things are not the same.
What hair I have is snowy white;
Left hip's kind of lame.

My campfire coals have glowed and cooled.

Ashes scattered to the wind.

The trail is getting shorter now,

Not long to the end.

But I love old Wyoming.

And I'm leaving her to you.

Enjoy but treat her gently, friend,

'Cause we're all just passin' through.

—by Howard Ballew (a friend of mine)

CHANGES

We have seen many changes as I finish writing this in the summer of 2003. More and more people have arrived and now the biggest challenge is for these people who want to live in this magnificent part of the West is to find property or housing they can afford. Real estate prices have skyrocketed! It was difficult when we moved here, because only 2.5 per cent of Teton County was (or is now) privately owned. Ninety seven point five per cent is in national forest, national park, national elk refuge et al.

The town of Jackson is surrounded by 3.5 million acres of forestland or in a mountain wilderness setting. There are few roads even today. I say Thanks Goodness for that!

In my 70's, I am still outfitting and guiding big game hunters, in the same Crystal Creek Camps. They come from all over the world. It's been more than 40 years since starting this lifestyle. My mind wanders...places my body can no longer go!

[Wixom note: Gap describes himself to others as an old bear who is content to lie on his back on a sunny day and gaze into his wilderness. Feeling the aches and pains of many hard years, working in all kinds of weather, he especially feels the bumps and bruises of outfitting and bronco busting during those years.]

It was especially hard for me when my two horses, veterans of the wilderness, passed away. Sunny Jim has been mentioned but I also lament the loss of Eagle, my proud Morgan horse who died Nov. 27, 2002, at age 27. I recall with fond memories how both horses carried me through thunderstorms, blizzards and lightning where I could often not even see my mount's ears! There were many miles of night riding where one had to rely on the horse's instincts to get me safely back to camp. They built my business and paid the bills. They were my friends. They will be sorely missed! Eagle, like Sunny, is buried here on the ranch. Along with my prize-winning black Morgan stallion, Starless Knight, mentioned earlier, I lost three of my personal horses in a three-month period. It darned near killed me!

I've had many adventures with wildlife, especially big game animals right here at our homestead. When it was 40 below zero, with three feet of snow, I like to remember feeding bighorn sheep from my hand. I've broken ice on the creek so that both horses and big game could drink.

Next door is the state refuge where the elk are fed; but the bighorn sheep also need help. I don't know why the state can't provide the sheep salt and feed them as well as the elk. Sometimes in tough winters mule deer wander by and get on the highway south of here along the Hoback River. At no time of year is this region so obviously a haven for big game animals as during the winter and they are quite vulnerable here at such times. It seems irresponsible to just let them suffer and die.

All big game populations, including elk, deer, moose and bighorn sheep, have declined in recent years—all except the predators! There seems to be more bears and mountain lions. Most are black bears but grizzles have been in the area as well, causing much concern over hunter safety. Now we have to worry about timber wolves introduced into the Yellowstone ecosystem. These elk-eating critters may spend the summer in Yellowstone but come deep snow and they are right here among us in Jackson Hole. What elk they don't eat they scare out of their wits. The elk are now difficult to keep on the feed lots. The wapiti are so spooked in Jackson Hole that they run from one feed refuge to another, with Canis lupis following. Without being able to use these feed lots, the elk won't survive. Even moose are on the run. The moose population is way down. All of the above spells less opportunity for hunters and for wildlife watchers in general.

One article in a Jackson Hole newspaper in the winter of 2010 described how a man took his pet lion hounds out for a run, and they were attacked by wolves. By the time the owner could ride up to them, three dogs had been killed and partially eaten.

While some would say wolves are simply trying to stay alive, they are also vicious eating machines. Nor do they always kill simply to survive. They often kill wantonly, leaving meat to waste.

If you took the same snowshoe hike I used to take, you would have seen hundreds of deer, elk and lots of moose, plus bighorn sheep. You could read of hundreds of wild game mentioned in my journals. But things have changed. More control is needed over the predators no matter what the WGFD or U.S. Fish and Wildlife Service says.

In addition, local zoning laws in many instances do not allow sufficient winter habitat for the game animals. More housing and commercial developments are being built along the foothills, with less food for starving deer and elk. People build where game once wintered and then complain that the animals, who were there first, are eating their fitzers. Officers are called in to scatter them, or even shoot them on land they have always used. Where is room for wildlife? Things will not get better by themselves. They will only get worse.

The WGFD and Forest Service are helping in one regard, by banning human trespass on wintering ranges around Jackson Hole. But we must ask if it is enough to protect the natural resource of such tremendous importance to the citizens of (and visitors to) Jackson Hole. But we must ask if it is enough for the rich quality of life values which with which Jackson Hole residents are so enamored: its wildlife.

I worry about the terrible inroads into our priceless wilderness. Roads are being cut where they shouldn't be...to look for oil and who knows what else. Research has proven conclusively that elk shun roads whenever possible. The terrible destruction of wildlife environment is unnecessary and the scars are going to last for a long time. Big game isn't getting more plentiful; sportsmen everywhere should be concerned about it no matter where they live.

All this has made things more difficult for the region's hunters and outfitters. Both the wolves and grizzlies are protected by federal law, so we can't even thin them out when they become too aggressive. As mentioned, one biologist told me, "You can, of course, shoot one in self defense but be prepared to show the bite marks on your leg."

While this may be a slight exaggeration, the point is that it is one more problem to deal with. Outfitters have enough of their own what with obtaining permits, bad weather, rough terrain, long distances, and excessive overhead expenses, etc.

Black bears and cougars can be hunted but there are set quotas and the outfitter must be careful to abide by state hunting regulations. Bears have not only poked holes in my tents but as related, torn them apart. Another outfitter farther north in Wyoming has said that every time a grizzly wanders near, he can expect to spend another $2,000 in tent and food replacement. One must also hope no humans are injured.

Maybe the time will come when wolves are no longer federally protected. It can be expected that when the population increases sufficiently, the state will take over management of Canis lupis from the feds. When that happens and wolves can be hunted, outfitters might have a chance to restore decreasing game populations.

Note: Coyotes can be pesky on the elk refuges but rarely make much of an inroad. Wolves, on the other hand, threaten new-born calves to such an extent that there may be little chance of herds increasing. And even if wolves do not kill elk outright, they follow elk from one refuge to another, it becomes difficult to see that they get the feed they need. In my opinion, it may be necessary to decide whether we want elk or protected wolves.

Here is what others say about the wolf dilemma:

Jackson Hole Outfitters and Guide Assn: "In one week, March 14-21, 2003, 13 elk were killed by wolves on the state feed grounds... in one night a lone wolf killed five calf elk on the Camp Creek feed grounds over a fence near where we live all winter long, eating only a small portion of two calves. There are no elk on the Fish Creek feed grounds, the wolves having driven them off. Some 25 elk are being killed each week in local feed lots...the cow-calf ratio on Gros Ventre is 18:100 this year. Traditionally, it is 32:100. This decline in calves has increased as the wolves increase. And as of this writing, it has gotten worse.

"Conclusion: we have a crisis looming...wildlife without sound management."

•••

Wixom note: Many magazine stories have been written about Pucci and his expertise in elk guiding/hunting and his knowledge of elk in general. In a story for *Outdoor Life*, Erwin Bauer told how he witnessed Gap bugle in two six-point bulls with a piece of plugged up rubber tubing. There have also been other stories about his ability to connect both bow and rifle hunters with trophy bull elk. Many marvel at his ability to pack out venison without panniers, just as mountain man Jim Bridger did it. Gap is known as a master packer in moving game and supplies by horseback over long distances in rugged wilderness. "It's all in the ropes," says Pucci. "If you are going to stay in the outfitting business, you keep learning until you do it right."

As such, Gap speaks for many others when he calls on local legislators to do something to protect one of northwestern Wyoming's most valuable resources. Federal elk managers have stated in the past that they want to maintain the Jackson Hole elk herds (some winter out of Yellowstone Park) from November to April in the National Elk Refuge at 7,500 animals. This is now being set at a lower quota. Wolves in Yellowstone just follow the elk to the refuges and make management difficult. Gap: "When they introduced wolves into Yellowstone, they said the wolves would not leave Yellowstone. What a joke! When the game animals go to lower elevations as they always do in winter, predators such as wolves are sure to follow."

The question is asked, how can managers keep the desired number intact with wolves running the wapiti off the feed grounds at such a critical time?

IN SUMMARY
by Hartt Wixom

———

A magazine article written by Sal and Bernadette Pitera several decades ago epitomize the Wild West Peggy and Gap have enjoyed. It begins like this: "In 1964 a Norristown, Pa. youth traveled to the V Bar V Ranch owned by Albert and Margaret Feuz in the fabled Jackson Hole valley of Wyoming for an elk and deer hunt. Having accomplished his hunting mission, Gap realized he hadn't bagged his limit...Gap set out to woo and pursue Peggy Ann McClung of Lawrence, Kansas and Salt Lake City, Utah.

"In the natural course of events, the young couple settled down in an old Pennsylvania Dutch farmhouse with a 40-acre spread, a couple of horses, and a moose rack on the barn. But the American dream wasn't enough to sustain them; frontiers beckoned and in 1973, they obliged."

The story then describes how the two migrated to the area in northwestern Wyoming that Gap had fallen in love with...and in time, Peggy did too. It wasn't really too much of a "sell," for Peggy was raised of pioneer stock moving by wagon train from Missouri in 1865. For a time her ancestors lived in Indian Territory, Oklahoma, before settling in Lawrence, Kansas and northern Utah. Peggy says it fulfilled her own dream in living out her pioneer legacy.

Peggy's prized diaries tell how she grew to love a life of adversity, for it was a challenge she and her husband were determined to meet. How well they did, readers can decide for themselves.

Catherine cooking hot dogs and beans at camp.

GAP AND PEG'S
RANCH AND CAMP RECIPES

French Toast

6 eggs
½ cup milk, or slightly more
1 Tbsp. sugar
dash cinnamon
dash salt
12-14 slices of bread

Beat eggs until blended, add milk and all other ingredients. Best to use flat-bottom bowl large enough for dipping bread slices.

Heat skillet or griddle until hot. Add margarine or some other fat. (Margarine gives best flavor.) Dip bread—stale bread works best if available—on both sides, allowing excess to drain back into bowl, and place on griddle. Watch heat to avoid burning. Turn to lightly brown on both sides.
Serves 6-7

Camp Coffee

1 heaping tablespoon coffee for each cup water. Put coffee and water in pot; bring to brisk boil. Remove from fire for four to five minutes, then put it back over the fire and let it come to a boil again (about 10-18 minutes).

Gap's Griddle Cakes

2 c. flour
2 Tbsp. sugar
¾ tsp. salt
3 tsp. baking powder
2 eggs
1 ½ c. milk
¼ c. melted shortening, margarine or oil

Mix all ingredients well and ladle into heated, greased skillet. Flip when bubbles appear in the batter.
(serves 4)

Camp Omelets

2 eggs per omelet
milk
dash of salt and pepper
filling of choice

Use small skillet for individual omelets (8-9") or place more eggs in a larger skillet and divide. (Too large an omelet will break.) Heat skillet over medium heat. Beat eggs slightly and add a little milk and a dash of salt and pepper.

When the skillet is hot, melt butter, bacon grease or other fat enough to cover bottom of pan. Test temperature of pan with drops of water; if they sizzle, pan is right.

Pour egg mixture in skillet and allow to set on bottom. Lift edges with knife or spatula; right temperature of pan will allow omelet to slide around skillet freely. When half set, add other ingredients— cheese, peppers, bacon, ham, etc. When almost completely set, fold omelet over itself and slide omelet from pan. Note: an omelet is never "turned over," but is completely cooked from one side.

Garnish with more vegetables, meat, tomato sauce, etc.

At Home on the Range
Peggy Pucci's Wild Game Stew

2 lbs. meat cut in large cubes. Use elk, moose, deer,
   antelope, buffalo, jackrabbit or "horse meat."
4 stalks celery, sliced
1 large onion, coarsely chopped
6 carrots, sliced
6 potatoes cut in large cubes
1 Tbsp. Kitchen Bouquet
1 12-oz. can stewed tomatoes
2 tsp. salt (or to taste)
¼ tsp. black pepper
dash chili powder
1 tsp. Worcestershire sauce
2 bouillon cubes
water

Brown meat in a little oil in a large cast iron pot. Add onion, stewed tomatoes, and enough water to cover generously. Simmer slowly until meat begins to get tender. Then add celery, carrots, seasonings, and potatoes. Add more water if necessary to cover. Continue to simmer. When potatoes become tender but not over-tender, mix 2-4 T. cornstarch with a little cold water to make a paste. Just before serving, stir just enough paste into simmering stew to make it the right consistency. If desired, make dumplings or biscuits to go on top of stew. Canned biscuits from the store also work well. After topping with dumplings or biscuits, brown in oven at 350° for 10-15 minutes or according to dumpling or biscuit recipe.

Camp Recipe
"Monument Peak Moose or Elk Braciola"
(Italian style steak rolls)

You'll love wild game cooked this way. You may also use deer or bighorn sheep steaks. This old Italian recipe has been used for generations by Gap's family and by Peggy.

Sauce Ingredients
> tomato sauce
> 2 T. bacon grease
> 1 lg. onion, chopped
> 2 cloves garlic, minced
> 2 12-oz. cans tomato paste
> salt and pepper
> 1 tsp. crushed oregano leaves
> 1 tsp. crushed basil leaves
> 1 tsp. rosemary, crumpled
> ¼ c. snipped fresh parsley
> 1 T. sugar
> 1 lb. ground moose or elk meat, or as much as desired.

To prepare: Sauté onion and garlic in grease in medium cast iron kettle. Do not brown. When tender, add tomato paste and stir. Fill 12 oz. empty tomato paste cans with hot water to equal five cans of water, adding to tomato paste one can at a time, stirring until smooth. Add seasonings, heat to simmering, then to low heat, stirring occasionally.

Steaks
> 3 lg. moose or elk round steaks, cut to 3/8 thick
> ¼ tsp. crushed oregano
> ¼ tsp. crushed rosemary
> ¼ tsp. crushed basil
> ¼ tsp. marjoram
> 4 to 5 T. fresh snipped parsley
> salt and pepper to taste

Spread large moose or elk round steaks on heavy pounding board. Using meat tenderizer, pound round steaks evenly to about ¼ inch. Sprinkle blended herbs, salt and pepper, parsley, grated cheese and bread crumbs evenly over each steak. Tightly roll up each steak, shorter end first, and tie securely with cord in three places and trim ends of cord.

Brown each steak roll in small amount of olive oil in cast iron skillet until brown on all sides, and transfer to kettle of simmering sauce. Simmer 3-4 hours, stirring often to prevent sauce from scorching. Keep covered for first couple of hours, then uncover partly so sauce thickens.

To serve: Remove each steak roll from sauce. Snip cord and remove from roll. Slice crosswise with very sharp knife about ½-inch thick piece. Arrange on large platter and drizzle with tomato sauce. Serve Italian Braciola (Steak Rolls) with your favorite pasta, sprinkled with grated Romano cheese.

Chili

1-2 large onions, chopped
1-2 cloves garlic, crushed or chopped,
    or about ¼ tsp. powdered garlic
3 lbs. or more ground meat
2 qts. canned tomatoes, or use 2 12-oz. cans tomato paste
    with 4 cans water
salt and pepper to taste
2-4 Tbsp. chili powder or more, to taste

Add small amount of oil or fat to dutch oven then add meat, onion and garlic. When the neat is browned, add remaining ingredients and simmer slowly 1-2 hours. When about ready to serve, add regular size cans of red or kidney beans.

Spaghetti Sauce

Up to ¼ c. oil or shortening
1 lg. onion, chopped
1 clove garlic, chopped, or use powdered
2 12-oz. cans tomato paste
4 cans water
salt and pepper to taste
1 Tbsp. sugar
¼ tsp. oregano

Fry onion and garlic in oil. Add tomato paste and stir. Gradually add each can of water and stir until smooth. Salt and pepper to taste. Add sugar and oregano and blend and simmer very slowly until smooth and of right consistency. Stir often.

Meat Sauce

Use very small amount of oil if using ground meat. Use spaghetti sauce recipe above, but when onion is partly cooked, add ground meat to brown. Add tomato paste and water and simmer as above.

Deer Heart with Tomato Sauce

Rinse heart well and place in kettle or pan. Cover with water, add 1 Tbsp. or more of salt to water. Bring to boil and simmer until tender to touch of fork. Remove from water and let cool. Slice cooked heart about 3/8" thick. Meanwhile, have tomato sauce simmering in pan or dutch oven. Place slices in sauce, stir, cover and simmer *slowly* until ready to serve, 30 minutes to 1 hour.

Simple Tomato Sauce

2 Tbsp. oil
½ to 1 lg. onion, chopped
1 or 2 lg. cans of stewed tomatoes, slightly mashed
salt, pepper and other seasonings (oregano and garlic OR chili
    powder to taste.

Simmer oil and onion slightly. Add tomatoes, which are slightly mashed, and stir. Add salt and pepper to taste, then seasonings. Stir and bring to simmering boil. Good for use with deer heart, pot roast. round steak, chicken, etc.

Spanish Rice

2 Tbsp. of oil, fat, bacon grease, etc.
½ to 1 c. onion, chopped
Meat, if desired: pork chops or meat strips or
    cubes of ham, beef, chicken or any game
1 c. regular rice
1 qt. canned tomatoes, mashed
1 tsp. salt (less if meat is salty)
1-2 tsp. chili powder
¼ tsp. pepper
dash garlic powder (or use fresh crushed and fry with onion)
¼ to ½ lb. cheese, shredded.

Fry onion in fat until tender. Add meat, if used, and brown slightly. Pour uncooked rice over meat, then sprinkle spices over the mixture. Stir around slightly. Add tomatoes and stir until rice and seasonings are blended in.

Cover, simmer slowly, stirring occasionally to bring rice off bottom. Test rice for doneness after moisture is absorbed (45-60 minutes).

May need to add more water and continue cooking slowly until done. Do not overcook, or rice becomes mushy.

Note: If using large pieces of meat, or if meat is tough, cook sufficiently beforehand to tenderize before adding to mixture.

CRYSTAL CREEK OUTFITTERS MENU

1. **Sliced Ham**
   Macaroni and cheese, green beans, bread, lemonade.
   Dessert: fruit cocktail

2. **Baked Chicken**
   Scalloped potatoes, mixed veggies, salad with dressing,
   bread. Dessert: make a cake

3. **Baked Pork Chops**
   Spanish rice, corn, applesauce, bread.
   Dessert: chocolate pudding

4. **Roast Beef with Gravy**
   Mashed potatoes, green beans, throw in carrots with roast,
   salad, bread. Dessert: cherry cobbler

5. **T-Bone Steaks**
   Baked potatoes, corn, salad, bread.
   Dessert: cake

6. **Roast Turkey with Gravy**
   Stove Top stuffing, mixed veggies, buttered rice, cranberry
   sauce, bread. Dessert: three pumpkin pies

7. Meatloaf with Gravy
Buttered noodles, green beans, bread, salad.
Dessert: peach crisp

8. Chicken Fried Steak with Gravy
Mashed potatoes, corn, bread.
Dessert: cake

9. Swiss Steaks with Diced Tomatoes and Onion
Spanish rice, mixed veggies, bread.
Dessert: Jell-O

Special Helps

Bread estimate:
22-24 sandwiches per day x 9 days high camp, plus
base camp 1st breakfast toast (2 loaves) and
base camp 1st day lunch (2-3 loaves)

Egg estimate (12 people / 10 day hunt)
2 doz. x 9 days high camp breakfasts plus
2 doz. for baking

Average quantities per meal (13-15 persons)
Jell-O: 2 large packages
Lemonade: 2 pkgs. per 1 cup sugar in each pitcher;
2 pitchers per meal
Most vegetables: 6 cans
Bacon: 2.5 - 3 packs
Sausage: 3 packs

PHOTO CREDITS

Bob Wuebler, pg. 146, top

David Staley, pg. 162, top

Ed Roberts, pg. 150, both

Elizabeth McCabe, pg. 164, bottom

Erwin Bauer, Cover; pg. 74, bottom; pg. 134, both; pg. 145, bottom; pg. 154, both;

Gap Pucci, pg. 75, both; pg. 78, bottom; pg. 80, bottom; pg. 135, top;
    pg. 142, bottom; pg. 155, bottom; pg. 156, top; pg. 157, top; pg. 158, bottom;
    pg. 159, both; pg. 210

Gwilliam Family, pg. 165, bottom

Hartt Wixom, pg. 132, bottom; pg. 133

Linda Roberts, pg. 136, top

Murray Burnam, pg. 132, top

Peggy Pucci, pg. 69, bottom; pg. 71; pg. 72, top; pg. 73, bottom; pg. 76-77, all;
    pg. 78, top; pg. 79, both; pg. 80, top; pg. 131; pg. 136, bottom; pg. 137-140;
    pg. 141; pg. 142, top; pg. 143, both; pg. 145, top; pg. 146, bottom; pg. 147,
    both; pg. 148-149, all; pg. 151, top; pg. 155, top; pg. 156, bottom;
    pg. 158, top; pg. 164, top; pg. 196; pg. 222

Sal Pitera, pg. 72, bottom; pg. 73, top; pg. 152, top

Teresa Pucci, pg. 144, bottom; pg. 151, top; pg. 162, bottom

Unknown, pg. 69, top; pg. 70, courtesy of Sal Pitera; pg. 74 top, courtesy of
    Sal Pitera; pg. 144, top; pg. 157, bottom; pg. 160-161, unknown client photos;
    pg. 164, courtesy of Sal Pitera

GODSPEED, FRIENDS.

From photo montage in Gap's home: We know that happiness is being healthy, with enough to eat, a warm bed, and a scrap of canvas to keep out the weather. It is good books to read, a camera and a pen with which to record interesting things. It is telling stories around the evening fires, with maybe a coyote howling somewhere in the background under the purple canopy of stars. It is watching campfire smoke lift in a twisting ribbon between sentinel spruce. It is meeting and knowing people from all corners of the world in such a setting, where all the frills and ginger-bread fall away, revealing men not as gods, but as truly a part of nature's pattern. Happiness is growing up in wild country where there are elk to hunt, fish to catch, horses to ride, and butterflies to watch. It is, above all things, laughter and love.